1,000,000 Books

are available to read at

Forgotten Books

www.ForgottenBooks.com

Read online
Download PDF
Purchase in print

ISBN 978-1-5279-1033-1
PIBN 10939707

This book is a reproduction of an important historical work. Forgotten Books uses state-of-the-art technology to digitally reconstruct the work, preserving the original format whilst repairing imperfections present in the aged copy. In rare cases, an imperfection in the original, such as a blemish or missing page, may be replicated in our edition. We do, however, repair the vast majority of imperfections successfully; any imperfections that remain are intentionally left to preserve the state of such historical works.

Forgotten Books is a registered trademark of FB &c Ltd.
Copyright © 2018 FB &c Ltd.
FB &c Ltd, Dalton House, 60 Windsor Avenue, London, SW19 2RR.
Company number 08720141. Registered in England and Wales.

For support please visit www.forgottenbooks.com

1 MONTH OF FREE READING

at

www.ForgottenBooks.com

By purchasing this book you are eligible for one month membership to ForgottenBooks.com, giving you unlimited access to our entire collection of over 1,000,000 titles via our web site and mobile apps.

To claim your free month visit:

www.forgottenbooks.com/free939707

* Offer is valid for 45 days from date of purchase. Terms and conditions apply.

English
Français
Deutsche
Italiano
Español
Português

www.forgottenbooks.com

Mythology Photography **Fiction**
Fishing Christianity **Art** Cooking
Essays Buddhism Freemasonry
Medicine **Biology** Music **Ancient Egypt** Evolution Carpentry Physics
Dance Geology **Mathematics** Fitness
Shakespeare **Folklore** Yoga Marketing
Confidence Immortality Biographies
Poetry **Psychology** Witchcraft
Electronics Chemistry History **Law**
Accounting **Philosophy** Anthropology
Alchemy Drama Quantum Mechanics
Atheism Sexual Health **Ancient History**
Entrepreneurship Languages Sport
Paleontology Needlework Islam
Metaphysics Investment Archaeology
Parenting Statistics Criminology
Motivational

English Reprints.

JOHN SELDEN.

TABLE-TALK.
1689.

περὶ παντὸς τὴν ἐλευθερίαν
(Above all things, Liberty).

CAREFULLY EDITED BY

EDWARD ARBER,
Associate, King's College, London, F.R G.S., &c.

LONDON :
ALEX. MURRAY & SON, 30, QUEEN SQUARE, W C
1 June, 1868.

Ent Stat. Hall.] ONE SHILLING. [*All Rights reserved.*]

CONTENTS.

CHRONICLE of the Life, Works, and Times, of John Selden   3

INTRODUCTION, ... 9

BIBLIOGRAPHY, ... 12

                  TABLE-TALK. . . . 13

1. The Table 14, 15

2. Dedication to Selden's Trustees, by Rev. Richard Milward, sometime his amanuensis . . . 16

3. THE DISCOURSES OF JOHN SELDEN, ESQ. . . 17—80

CHRONICLE
of
fome of the principal events
in the
LIFE, WORKS, and TIMES
of
JOHN SELDEN.
Antiquary, Philologist, Heraldist, Linguist, Jurist, Statesman, &c.

* Probable or approximate dates.

A Life of Selden does not exist: to the great reproach of the Lawyers. All accounts of him are but sketches.
Few of Selden's many works have been mentioned here, for want of space. A list of them is given in Dr. Aikin's *Life of Selden*, pp. 197-9. Ed. 1812.

1558. Nov. 17. Elizabeth begins to reign.

Birth and Infancy.

1584. Dec. 16.

JOHN SELDEN, the glory of the English nation, as Hugo Grotius worthily stiles him, son of John Selden, by Margaret his wife, the only daughter of Thomas Baker of Rushington, (descended from the knightly family of the Bakers in Kent) was born in an obscure village called Salvington near to Terring a market town in Sussex. His father . . . . was a sufficient plebeian, and delighted much in music, by the exercising of which he obtained (as 'tis said) his wife, of whom our famous author Jo. Selden was born on the 16th of Decemb. 1584. *Wood, Ath. Oxon.* iii. 366. Ed. 1817.

The birthplace of John Selden is Salvington, a hamlet of the parish of West Tarring, in the county of Sussex. Tarring is about two miles from Worthing. . . . The cottage in which he was born still remains. It was then known as Lacies, being the residence attached to a farm of about eighty-one acres. The date of 1601 is upon its front. *G. W. Johnson. Memoirs of John Selden*, pp. 33, 34. Ed. 1835.

Dec. 20. '1584—John, the sonne of John Selden, the minstrell, was baptized the 20th day of December.' *Parish Register of West Tarring.*

Besides John there were two younger sons, who died infants, and a daughter, who married to a John Bernard of Goring in Sussex: by whom she had two sons and four daughters. They appear to have remained in humble situations. *Johnson, idem.*

At Chichester School.

1594. æt. 10.

He was 'instructed in grammar learning in the Free School at Chichester, under Mr. Hugh Barker of New College [Oxford].' *Wood, idem.*

On the inside of the lintel of his birthplace and home "is carved a Latin distich, said to have been composed by Selden when only ten years old. . . . The following literal copy made at the time of a personal inspection [in August 1834] is submitted to the reader's judgement.

GRATVS HOneste MIH' NO ClAVDAR INITIO SEDEB'
FVR ABEAS: NO SV FACTA SOLVTA TIBI.

The last character of the first line is somewhat imperfect. It probably was intended as a contraction of ' que.' In this case the literal translation is ' Honest friend thou art welcome to me, I will not be closed, enter and be seated. Thief! begone, I am not open to thee.'"
Johnson, idem.

with *ita est*, and *subscription of his name*. Then was it printed, and until it was wholly printed, I never had the least expression of any dislike to it from any man that had any *authority* or *power of command*, either in the *state*, or in the church.—*Omnia opera*, iii. 1456.

Dec. The king, who had no knowledge of Selden but through the misrepresentations of his courtiers, summoned him by his secretary, Sir Robert Naunton, to appear, with his work, at the Palace of Theobalds. 'I,' says Selden, 'being then entirely a stranger to the court, and known personally there to a very few, was unwilling to go thither unaccompanied,' and consequently he obtained the attendance of his old friend and fellow-templar, Edward Heyward, of Reepham, in Norfolk, and of Ben Jonson, 'princeps poetarum,' to introduce him to the king. . . . Selden had two conferences with King James at Theobald's, and one at Whitehall, and bears testimony in several parts of his after-writings to the ability and courtesy of his Majesty.—*Johnson*, pp. 64, 67.

1619. Jan. 28. æt. 34. Selden however is cited before the High Commission Court at Lambeth Palace. One of his opponents, Dr. Richard Tillesley, Archdeacon of Rochester, in his *Animadversions upon Mr. Selden's History of Tythes and his Review thereof*, 2nd Edition, 1621, triumphantly quotes the following:—

His submission because he denieth to haue beene *in the High Commission Court*, and for that in my *Answere to his Pamphlet* it is not so perfitly related, may it please thee Reader, here to reade it whole out of the Registry of that Court.

Vicesimo octauo die Mensis Ianuarij, Anno Domini iuxta computationem Ecclesiæ Anglicanæ 1618. *Coram Reuerendissimo in Christo patre, Domino Georgio, prouidentia diuina Cantuariensi Archiepiscopo, totius Angliæ Primate et Metropolitano, Iohanne London, Lancelot Winton, et Iohanne Roffen, eadem prouidentia respectiuè Episcopis: Iohanne Bennet, Willielmo Bird et Georgio Newman, Militibus, in Manerio Archiepiscopali apud Lambehith in Comitatu Surrey, iudicialiter sedentibus: præsente Thoma Mottershed.*

Officium Dominorum contra Iohannem Selden de Interiori Templo London, Armigerum.

This day appeared personally *Iohn Selden* Esquire, and made his submission all vnder his owne hand writing, touching the publication of his Booke entituled *The History of Tithes, Sub tenore verborum sequente*.

"My good Lords, I most humbly acknowledge my errour, which I haue committed in publishing the *History of Tithes*, and especially, in that I have at all by shewing any interpretation of Holy Scriptures, by medling with Councels, Fathers, or Canons, or by what elsesoeuer occurres in it, offered any occasion of Argument against any right of Maintenance *Iure Diuino* of the Ministers of the Gospell: Beseeching your Lordships to receiue this ingenuous and humble acknowledgement, together with the vnfeigned protestation of my griefe, for that through it I haue so incurred both his Maiesties and your Lordships displeasure conceiued against mee in the behalfe of the Church of England.—*Iohn Selden*."

The High Commission Court suppress his book.

This 'usage sunk so deep into his stomach, that he did

CHRONICLE.

sayd he, 'I never knew a wise man make a wise will.'

Death. 1654. Nov. 30. æt. 69. John Selden dies at White Friars, of dropsy.
Dec. 14. Is magnificently buried in the Temple church. His executors 'invited all the parliament men, all the benchers, and great officers. All the judges had mourning, as also an abundance of persons of quality.' Archbishop Usher preached his funeral sermon.

We may adduce the testimony of three contemporaries:—

1. G. Berkeley, Earl of Berkeley, in his *Historical Applications and occasional Meditations upon several subjects. Written by a Person of Honour.* London 1670, p. 12. gives us the following—

Our Learned *Selden*, before he dyed, sent for the most Reverend Arch-Bishop *Usher*, and the Rev. Dr. *Langbaine*, and discoursed to them of this purpose; *That he had survey'd most part of the Learning that was among the Sons of Men; that he had his Study full of Books and Papers of most Subjects in the world; yet at that time he could not recollect any passage out of infinite Books and Manuscripts he was Master of, wherein he could Rest his Soul, save out of the Holy Scriptures; wherein the most remarkable passage that lay most upon his spirit was* Titus ii. 11, 12, 13, 14.

2. E. Hyde, Lord Clarendon, in his Autobiography, written about 20 years after Selden's death, gives the following character of him, in which may be traced admiration for his character and abilities; and regret, it may be sneering resentment, at his choosing the side of the Parliament in the Civil War.

"Mr. SELDEN was a Person, whom no Character can flatter, or transmit in any expressions equal to his Merit and Virtue: He was of so stupendous Learning in all Kinds, and in all Languages (as may appear in his excellent and transcendent Writings) that a man would have thought He had been entirely conversant amongst Books, and had never spent an Hour but in Reading and Writing; yet his Humanity, Courtesy, and Affability was such, that He would have been thought to have been bred in the best Courts, but that his good Nature, Charity, and Delight in doing good, and in communicating all He knew, exceeded his Breeding: His Stile in all his Writings seems harsh and sometimes obscure; which is not wholly to be imputed to the abstruse Subjects of which He commonly treated, out of the Paths trod by other Men; but to a little vndervaluing the Beauty of a Stile, and too much Propensity to the Language of Antiquity; but in his Conversation He was the most clear Discourser, and had the best Faculty in making hard Things easy, and presenting them to the Understanding, of any Man that hath been known. Mr. *Hyde* was wont to say, that He valued himself upon nothing more than upon having had Mr. *Selden*'s Acquaintance from the Time He was very young; and held it with great Delight as long as They were suffered to continue together in *London;* and He was very much troubled always when He heard him blamed, censured, and reproached, for staying in *London,* and in the Parliament, after They were in Rebellion, and in the worst Times, which his Age obliged him to do; and how wicked soever the Actions were, which were every Day done, He was confident He had not given his Consent to them; but would have hindered them if He could, with his own Safety, to which He was always enough indulgent. If He had some Infirmities with other Men, they were weighed down with wonderful and prodigious Abilities and Excellencies in the other Scale."—*Life,* p. 16. *Ed.* 1759.

3. Rev. Richard Baxter, in his *Additional Notes on the Life and Death of Sir Matthew Hale. Kt.* London 1682. p. 40, thus writes:—

"I know you are acquainted, how greatly he [Sir M. Hale] valued Mr. *Selden,* being one of his Executors; his Books and Picture being still near him. I think it meet therefore to remember, that because many *Hobbists* do report, that Mr. *Selden* was at the heart an Infidel, and inclined to the Opinions of *Hobbs,* I desired him [Sir M. Hale] to tell me the truth herein; And he oft professed to me, that Mr. *Selden* was a resolved serious Christian; and that he was a great adversary to *Hobbs* his errors; and that he had seen him openly oppose him so earnestly, as either to depart from him, or drive him out of the Room."

These Sayings were publifhed thirty-five years after Selden's death, and nine years after their recorder— the Rev. Richard Milward, S.T.P., who died Canon of Windfor, Rector of Great Braxted, and Vicar of Isleworth—had paffed away. While they are, therefore, thus doubly pofthumous in publication, they muft be long antedated in utterance. *Table-Talk* belongs chiefly, if not entirely, to 1634—1654, and therefore appertains to the firft rather than the fecond half of the Seventeenth century.

These Difcourfes fhow fomewhat of the mind, but not the whole mind of Selden, even in the fubjects treated of. What muft have been the fulnefs of information, the aptnefs of illuftration, the love of truth, the juftnefs of reafoning, when fuch fragments as thefe could be picked up by a cafual hearer? Bacon's *Effays* are moft carefully finifhed compofitions: Selden's *Table-Talk* is the fpontaneous incidental outpouring of an overflowing mind; and yet it may not unworthily compare with the former.

Paffing by acute infight into human nature, and great antiquarian refearch, can we gather, however imperfectly, from the prefent work, any idea as to what Selden's main opinions were? We think we may.

In this work, as elfewhere, John Selden is the Champion of Human Law. It fell to his lot to live in a time when the life of England was convulfed, for years together, beyond precedent; when men fearched after the ultimate and effential conditions and frames of human fociety; when each ftrove fiercely for his *rights*, and then as dogmatically afferted them.

Amidft immenfe, prepofterous, and inflated affumptions; through the horrid tyranny of the fyftem of the *Thorough;* in the exciting debates of Parliament; in all the ftorm of the Civil War; in the ftill fiercer jarring of religious fects; amidft all the phenomena of that age; Selden clung to 'the Law of the Kingdom.' '*All is as the* State pleafes.' He advocates the supremacy of Human Law againſt the ſo-called doctrine of Divine Right. He thruſts out the Civil Power againſt all Eccleſiaſtical pretenſions, and raiſing it to be the higheſt authority in the State, denies the exiſtence of any other co-ordinate power. So ſtrongly does he aſſert the power of the Nation to do or not to do, that, for the purpoſe of his argument, he reduces Religion almoſt to a habit of thought, to be aſſumed or caſt off, like a faſhion in dreſs, at will. 'So Religion was brought into kingdoms, ſo it has been continued, and ſo it may be caſt out, when the State pleaſes.'* 'The Clergy tell the Prince they have Phyſick good for his Soul, and good for the Souls of his People, upon that he admits them: but when he finds by Experience they both trouble him and his People, he will have no more to do with them, what is that to them or any body elſe if a King will not go to Heaven'† 'The State ſtill makes the Religion and receives into it, what will beſt agree with it.'§

Selden lodges the Civil Power of England, in the King and the Parliament. He ſhews that our Engliſh Conſtitution is but one great Contract between two equal Princes, the Sovereign and the People; and that if that Contract be broken, both parties are at parity again. That, by a like conſent, the majority in England governs; the minority aſſenting to the judgement of the majority, and being involved in their deciſion. Finally, reducing all relationſhips to like mutual Agreements, he urges the keeping of Contracts, as the eſſential bond of Human ſociety. 'Keep your Faith.'

The way theſe views are enforced, fully juſtifies Lord Clarendon's opinion of him, that 'in his Converſation He was the moſt clear Diſcourſer, and had the beſt Faculty in making hard Things eaſy, and preſenting them to the Underſtanding, of any Man that hath been known.'‡

* P. 29. † P. 36. § P. 130. ‡ P. 8.

Table-Talk:

BEING THE

DISCOURSES

OF

John Selden, Efq.;

OR HIS

SENCE

Of Various

MATTERS

OF

WEIGHT and High CONSEQUENCE

Relating especially to

Religion and State.

Diſtingue Tempora.

LONDON,
Printed for *E. Smith*, in the Year MDCLXXXIX.

THE TABLE.

Abbeys, Priories, &c.	17
Articles, Baptifm,	18
Baftard, Bible, Scripture,	19
Bifhops before the Parliament,	22
Bifhops in the Parliament,	23
Bifhops out of the Parliament,	27
Books, Authors,	30
Cannon Laws, Ceremony,	31
Chancellor, Changing Sides,	32
Chriftmas, Chriftians,	33
Church,	34
Church of Rome, Churches,	35
City, Clergy,	36
High Commiffion, Houfe of Commons,	37
Confeffion, Competency,	38
Great Conjunction, Confcience,	39
Confecrated Places, Contracts,	40
Council, Convocation,	41
Creed, Damnation,	42
Devils,	43
Self-Denyal,	44
Duell,	45
Epitaph, Equity,	46
Evil-Speaking, Excommunication,	47
Faith and Works, Fafting-days,	48
Fathers and Sons, Fines, Free-will,	50
Fryers, Friends, Genealogy of Chrift,	51
Gentlemen, Gold,	52
Hall, Hell,	53
Holy-days, Humility, Idolatry, Jews,	54
Invincible Ignorance, Images,	55
Imperial Conftitution, Imprifonment, Incendiaries,	56
Independency, Things Indifferent, Publick Intereft,	57
Humane Invention, Judgements,	58
Judge, Juggling, Jurifdiction,	59
Jus Divinum, King,	60
King of England,	61
The King	62

THE TABLE.

Knights-Service, Land, Language,	64
Law,	65
Law of Nature, Learning,	66
Lecturers, Libels,	67
Liturgy, Lords in the Parliament,	68
Lords before the Parliament, Marriage,	69
Marriage of Cousin-Germans, Measure of Things,	70
Differences of Men, Minister Divine,	71
Money,	75
Moral Honesty, Mortgage, Number,	76
Oaths,	77
Oracles, Opinion,	79
Parity, Parliament,	80
Parson, Patience, Peace,	82
Penance, People, Pleasure,	83
Philosophy,	84
Poetry,	85
Pope,	86
Popery, Power, State,	88
Prayer,	90
Preaching,	91
Predestination,	95
Preferment,	96
Præmunire, Prerogative,	97
Presbytery,	98
Priests of Rome, Prophecies,	99
Proverbs, Question, Reason,	100
Retaliation, Reverence, Non-Residency,	101
Religion,	102
Sabboth, Sacrament,	105
Salvation, State, Superstition,	106
Subsidies, Simony, Ship-Money, Synod, Assembly,	107
Thanksgiving, Tythes,	109
Trade,	110
Tradition, Transubstantiation, Traitor, Trinity,	111
Truth, Trial,	112
University, Vows,	113
Usury, Pious Uses, War,	114
Witches,	116
Wife, Wisedom,	117
Wit, Women,	118
Year,	119
Zelots,	120

To the Honourable

Mr. Juſtice Hales,[*]

One of the JUDGES

OF THE

Common-Pleas;

And to the much Honoured

EDWARD HEYWOOD,[*] *IOHN VAUGHAN* and *ROWLAND JEWKS*, Eſquires.

Moſt worthy Gentlemen,

WEre you not Executors to that Perſon, who (while he liv'd) was the Glory of the Nation; yet I am Confident any thing of his would find Acceptance with you, and truly the Senſe and Notion here is wholy his, and moſt of the words. I had the opportunity to hear his Diſcourſe twenty Years together, and leaſt all thoſe Excellent things that uſually fell from him might be loſt, ſome of them from time to time I faithfully committed to Writing, where here digeſted into this Method, I humbly preſent to your Hands; you will quickly perceive them to be his by the familiar Illuſtrations wherewith they are ſet off, and in which way you know he was ſo happy, that (with a marvelous delight to thoſe that heard him) he would preſently convey the higheſt Points of Religion, and the moſt important Affairs of State to an ordinary apprehenſion.

In reading be pleaſed to diſtinguiſh Times, and in your Fancy carry along with you, the When *and the* Why, *many of theſe things were ſpoken; this will give them the more Life, and the ſmarter Reliſh. Tis poſſible the Entertainment you find in them, may render you the more inclinable to pardon the Preſumption of*

Your moſt Obliged and
moſt Humble Servant,
RI: MILWARD.

[*] *Miſprints for Mr. Juſtice Hale and Edward Heyward: see p. 7.*

THE
DISCOURSES
OF
John Selden, Efq;

Abbeys, Priories, &c.

1. THE unwillingnefs of the Monks to part with their Land, will fall out to be juft nothing, becaufe they were yielded up to the King by a Supream Hand (*viz.*) a Parliament. If a King conquer another Country, the People are loth to loofe their Lands, yet no Divine will deny, but the King may give them to whom he pleafe. If a Parliament make a Law concerning Leather, or any other Commodity, you and I for Example are Parliament Men, perhaps in refpect to our own private Interefts, we are againft it, yet the Major part conclude it, we are then involv'd and the Law is good.

2. When the Founder of Abbies laid a Curfe upon thofe that fhould take away thofe Lands, I would fain know what Power they had to curfe me; 'Tis not the Curfes that come from the Poor, or from any body, that hurt me, becaufe they come from them, but becaufe I do fomething ill againft them that deferves God fhould curfe me for it. On the other fide 'tis not a man's Bleffing me that makes me bleffed, he only declares me to be fo, and if I do well I fhall be bleffed, whether any blefs me or not.

3. At the time of Diffolution, they were tender in taking from the Abbots and Priors their Lands and their Houfes, till they furrendred them (as moft of

them did) indeed the Prior of St. *John's*, Sir *Richard Weston*, being a stout Man, got into *France*, and stood out a whole year, at last submitted, and the King took in that Priory also, to which the Temple belonged, and many other Houses in *England*, they did not then cry no Abbots, no Priors, as we do now no Bishops, no Bishops.

4. *Henry* the Fifth put away the Friars, Aliens, and seiz'd to himself 100000*l.* a year, and therefore they were not the Protestants only that took away Church Lands.

5. In Queen *Elisabeths* time, when all the Abbies were pulled down, all good Works defaced, then Preachers must cry up Justification by Faith, not by good Works.

Articles.

1. THE nine and thirty Articles are much another thing in Latin, (in which Tongue th made), then they are translated into English, they were made at three several Convocations, and confirmed by Act of Parliament six or seven times after. There is a Secret concerning them: Of late Ministers have subscribed to all of them, but by Act of Parliament that confirm'd them, they ought only to subscribe to those Articles which contain matter of Faith, and the Doctrine of the Sacraments, as appears by the first Subscriptions. But Bishop *Bancroft* (in the Convocation held in King *James*'s days) he began it, that Ministers should subscribe to three things, to the Kings Supremacy, to the Common-prayer, and to the Thirty nine Articles; many of them do not contain matter of Faith. Is it matter of Faith how the Church should be govern'd? Whether Infants should be Baptized Whether we have any Property in our Goods? *&c.*

Baptism.

1. ' a good way to perswade men to be stned, to tell them that they had a Foulness about them, *viz.* Original Sin, that not be washed away but by Baptism.

2. *The* Baptizing of Children with us, does only

prepare a Child againſt he comes to be a Man, to underſtand what Chriſtianity means. In the Church of *Rome* it hath this effect, it frees Children from Hell. They ſay they go into *Limbus Infantum*. It ſucceeds Circumciſion, and we are ſure the Child underſtood nothing of that at eight days old; why then may not we as reaſonably baptiſe a Child at that Age? in *England* of late years I ever thought the Parſon baptiz'd his own Fingers rather than the Child.

3. In the Primitive times they had God-fathers to ſee the Children brought up in the Chriſtian Religion, becauſe many times, when the Father was a Chriſtian, the Mother was not, and ſometimes when the Mother was a Chriſtian, the Father was not, and therefore they made choice of two or more that were Chriſtians, to ſee their Children brought up in that Faith.

Baſtard.

1. 'TIS ſaid the 23d. of *Deuteron*. 2. [*A Baſtard ſhall not enter into the Congregation of the Lord, even to the tenth Generation.*] *Non ingredietur in Eccleſiam Domini*, he ſhall not enter into the Church. The meaning of the Phraſe is, he ſhall not marry a Jewiſh woman. But upon this groſly miſtaken; a Baſtard at this day in the Church of *Rome*, without a Diſpenſation, cannot take Orders; the thing haply well enough, where 'tis ſo ſetled; but 'tis upon a Miſtake (the Place having no reference to the Church) appears plainly by what follows at the third Verſe [*An Ammonite or Moabite ſhall not enter into the Congregation of the Lord, even to the tenth Generation.*] No you know with the Jews an Ammonite, or a Moabite could never be a Prieſt, becauſe their Prieſts were born ſo, not made.

Bible, Scripture.

1. 'TIS a great queſtion how we know Scripture to be Scripture, whether by the Church, or by Mans private Spirit. Let me aſk you how I know anything? how I know this Carpet to be Green? Firſt, becauſe ſomebody told me it was

Green; that you call the Church in your Way. Then after I have been told it is green, when I see that Colour again, I know it to be Green, my own Eyes tell me it is Green, that you call the private Spirit.

2. The English Translation of the Bible, is the best Translation in the World, and renders the Sense of the Original best, taking in for the English Translation, the Bishops Bible, as well as King *James*'s. The Translation in King *James*'s time took an excellent way. That part of the Bible was given to him who was most excellent in such a Tongue (as the *Apochrypha* to *Andrew Downs*) and then they met together, and one read the Translation, the rest holding in their Hands some Bible, either of the learned Tongues, or *French, Spanish, Italian*, &c. if they found any Fault they spoke, if not, he read on.

3. There is no Book so translated as the Bible for the purpose. If I translate a *French* Book into *English*, I turn it into *English* Phrase, not into *French English* [*Il fait froid*] I say 'tis cold, not, it makes cold, but the Bible is rather translated into *English* Words, than into *English* Phrase. The Hebraisms are kept, and the Phrase of that Language is kept: As for Example [he uncovered her Shame] which is well enough, so long as Scholars have to do with it; but when it comes among the Common People, Lord, what Gear do they make of it!

4. *Scrutamini Scripturas.* These two Words have undone the World, because Christ spake it to his Disciples, therefore we must all, Men, Women and Children, read and interpret the Scripture.

5. *Henry* the Eighth made a Law, that all Men might read the Scripture, except Servants, but no Woman, except Ladies and Gentlewomen, who had Leisure, and might ask somebody the meaning. The Law was repealed in *Edward* the Sixth's days.

6. Lay-men have best interpreted the hard places in the Bible, such as *Johannes Picus, Scaliger, Grotius, Salmansius, Heinsius*, &c.

7. If you ask which of *Erasmus, Beza*, or *Grotius*

did beſt upon the New Teſtament, 'tis an Idle queſtion, for they all did well in their way. *Erafmus* broke down the firſt Brick, *Beza* added many things, and *Grotius* added much to him, in whom we have either ſomething new, or ſomething heightned, that was ſaid before, and ſo 'twas neceſſary to have them all three.

8. The Text ſerves only to gueſs by, we muſt ſatisfie our ſelves fully out of the Authors that liv'd about thoſe times.

9. In interpreting the Scripture, many do, as if a man ſhould ſee one have ten pounds, which he reckoned by 1. 2. 3. 4. 5. 6. 7. 8. 9. 10. meaning four, was but four Unities, and five, five Unities, &c. and that he had in all but ten pounds; the other that fees him, takes not the Figures together as he doth, but picks here and there, and thereupon reports, that he hath five pounds in one Bag, and ſix pounds in another Bag, and nine pounds in another Bag, &c. when as in truth he hath but ten pounds in all. So we pick out a Text here, and there to make it serve our turn; whereas, if we take it all together, and confider'd what went before, and what followed after, we ſhould find it meant no ſuch thing.

10. Make no more Allegories in Scripture than needs muſt, the Fathers were too frequent in them, they indeed, before they fully underſtood the litteral Sence, look'd out for an Allegory. The Folly whereof you may conceive thus; here at the firſt fight appears to me in my Window, a Glaſs and a Book, I take it for granted 'tis a Glaſs and a Book, thereupon I go about to tell you what they ſignifie; afterwards, upon nearer view, they prove no ſuch thing, one is a Box made like a Book, the other is a Picture made like a Glaſs, where's now my Allegory?

11. When Men meddle with the Litteral Text, the queſtion is, where they ſhould ſtop; in this caſe a Man might venture his Difcretion, and do his beſt to ſatisfie himſelf and others in thoſe places where he doubts, for although we call the Scripture the Word of God (as it is) yet it was writ by a Man, a mercenary

Man, whofe Copy, either might be falfe, or he might make it falfe: For Example, here were a thoufand Bibles printed in *England* with the Text thus, [*Thou fhalt commit Adultery*] the Word [*not*] left out; might not this Text be mended?

12. The Scripture may have more Senfes befides the Literal, becaufe God underftands all things at once, but a Man's Writing has but one true Sence, is that which the Author meant when he

13. When you meet with feveral Readings of the Text, take heed you admit nothing againft the Tenets of your Church, but do as if you were going over a Bridge, be fure you hold faft by the Rail, and then you may dance here and there as you pleafe, be fure you keep to what is fetled, and then you may flourifh upon your various Lections.

14. The *Apochrypha* is bound with the Bibles of all Churches that have been hitherto. Why fhould we leave it out? the Church of *Rome* has her *Apochrypha* (*viz.*) *Sufanna* and *Bell and the Dragon*, which she does not efteem equally with the reft of thofe Books that we call *Apochrypha*.

Bishops before the Parliament.

1. A Bifhop as a Bifhop, had never any Ecclefiaftial Jurifdiction; for as foon as he was *Electus Confirmatus*, that is, after the three Proclamations in *Bow-Church*, he might exercife Jurifdiction, before he was confecrated, not till then, he was no Bifhop, neither could he give Orders. Befides, *Suffragans* were Bifhops, and they never claim'd any Jurifdiction.

2. Antiently, the Noble Men lay within the City for Safety and Security. The Bifhops Houfes were by the Water-fide, becaufe they were held Sacred Ferfons ch no body would hurt.

3. There was fome Sence for *Commendams* at firft, when there was a Living void, and never a Clerk it, the Bifhops was to keep it till they found a fit Man, but now 'tis a Trick for the Bifhop to keep it for himfelf.

that were in ufage in this Kingdom, fhould be in force till the thirty two Commiffioners appointed fhould make others, provided they were not contrary to the Kings Supremacy. Now the Queftion will be, whether thefe Cannons for Blood were in ufe in this Kingdom or no? the contrary whereof may appear by many Prefidents, in *R*. 3. and *H*. 7. and the beginning of *H*. 8. in which time there were more attainted than fince, or fcarce before: The Cannons of Irregularity of Blood were never received in *England*, but upon pleafure. If a Lay Lord was attainted, the Bifhops affented to his Condemning, and were always prefent at the paffing of the Bill of Attainder: But if a Spiritual Lord, they went out as if they cared not whofe Head was cut off, fo none of their own. In thofe days the Bifhops being of great Houfes, were often entangled with the Lords in Matters of Treafon. But when d'ye hear of a Bifhop a Traytor now?

5. You would not have Bifhops meddle with Temporal Affairs, think who you are that fay it. If a Papift, they do in your Church; if an *Englifh* Proteftant, they do among you; if a Presbiterian, where you have no Bifhops, you mean your Presbiterian Lay Elders fhould meddle with Temporal Affairs as well as Spiritual. Befides, all Jurifdiction is Temporal, and in no Church, but they have fome Jurifdiction or other. The Queftion then will be reduced to *Magis* and *Minis;* they meddle more in one Church than in another.

6. *Objection*. Bifhops give not their Votes by Blood in Parliament, but by an Office annext to them, which being taken away, they ceafe to vote, therefore there is not the fame reafon for them as for Temporal Lords. *Anfw*. We do not pretend they have that Power the fame way, but they have a Right: He that has an Office in *Weftminfter-Hall* for his Life, the Office is as much his, as his Land is his that hath Land by Inheritance.

7. Whether had the inferior Clergy ever any thing to do in the Parliament? *Anfw*. No, no otherwife

than thus, There were certain of the Clergy that ufed to affemble near the Parliament, with whom the Bifhops, upon occafion might confult (but there were none of the Convocation, as 'twas afterwards fetled, (*viz.*) the Dean, the Arch-Deacon, one for the Chapter, and two for the Diocefs) but it hapned by continuance of time (to fave Charges and Trouble) their Voices and the Confent of the whole Clergy were involved in the Bifhops, and at this day the Bifhops Writs run, to bring all thefe to the Parliament, but the Bifhops themfelves ftand for all.

8. Bifhops were formerly one of thefe two Conditions, either Men bred Canonifts and Civilians, fent up and down Ambaffadors to *Rome* and other Parts, and fo by their Merit came to that Greatnefs, or elfe great Noble Mens Sons, Brothers, and Nephews, and fo born to govern the State : Now they are of a low Condition, their Education nothing of that way ; he gets a Living, and then a greater Living, and then a greater then that, and fo comes to govern.

9. Bifhops are now unfit to Govern becaufe of their Learning, they are bred up in another Law, they run to the Text for fomething done amongft the *Jews* that nothing concerns *England*, 'tis juft as if a Man would have a Kettle and he would not go to our *Brasier* to have it made ; as they make Kettles, but he would have it made as *Hiram* made his Brafs work, who wrought in *Solomons* Temple.

10. To take away Bifhops Votes, is but the beginning to take them away; for then they can be no longer ufeful to the King or State. 'Tis but like the little Wimble, to let in the greater Auger. *Objection.* But they are but for their Life, and that makes them always go for the King as he will have them. *Anfwer.* This is againft a double Charity, for you muft always fuppofe a bad King and bad Bifhops. Then again, whether will a Man be fooner content, himfelf fhould be made a Slave or his Son after him? [when we talk of our Children we mean our felves] befides they that have pofterity are more obliged to the King, then

they that are only for themfelves, in all the reafon in the World.

11. How fhall the Clergy be in the Parliament if the Bifhops are taken away? *Anfwer.* By the Layety, becaufe the Bifhops in whom the reft of the Clergy are included, are fent to the taking away their own Votes, by being involv'd in the major part of the Houfe. This follows naturally.

12. The Bifhops being put out of the Houfe, whom will they lay the fault upon now? When the Dog is beat out of the Room, where will they lay the ftink?

Bishops out of the Parliament.

1. IN the beginning Bifhops and Presbyters were alike, like the Gentlemen in the Country, whereof one is made Deputy Livetenant, another Juftice of Peace, fo one is made a Bifhop, another a Dean; and that kind of Government by Arch-Bifhops, and Bifhops no doubt came in, in imitation of the Temporal Government, not *Jure Divino.* In time of the *Roman* Empire, where they had a Legatus there they placed an Arch-Bifhop, where they had a Rector there a Bifhop, that every one might be inftructed in Chriftianity, which now they had received into the Empire.

2. They that fpeak ingenioufly of Bifhops and Presbyters, fay, that a Bifhop is a great Presbyter, and during the time of his being Bifhop, above a Prefbyter: as your Prefident of the Colledge of Phifitians, is above the reft, yet he himfelf is no more than a Doctor of Phyfick.

3. The words [Bifhop and Presbyter] are promifcuoufly ufed, that is confeffed by all, and though the word [Bifhop] be in *Timothy* and *Titus*, yet that will not prove the Bifhops ought to have a Jurifdiction over the Presbyter, though *Timothy* and *Titus* had by the order that was given them: fome Body muft take care of the reft, and that Jurifdiction was but to Excommunicate, and that was but to tell them they fhould come no more into their Company. Or grant they did make Canons one for another, before they came to

be in the State, does it follow they
the State has receiv'd them into it? What if *Timothy*
had Power in *Ephefus*, and *Titus* in *Creet* over the
Presbyters? Does it follow therefore the Bifhop muft
have the fame in *England*? Muft we be govern'd
like *Ephefus* and *Creet*?

4. However fome of the Bifhops pretend to be *Jure
Divino*, yet the Practice of the Kingdom had ever
been otherwife, for whatever Bifhops do othe
then the Law permits, *Weftminfter-Hall* can controul,
or fend them to abfolve, &c.

5. He that goes about to prove Bifhop
does as a Man that having a Sword fhall ftrike it
againft an Anvil, if he ftrike it a while there, he may
peradventure loofen it, though it be never fo well
riveted, 'twill ferve to ftrike another Sword (or cut
Flefh) but not againft an Anvil.

6. If you fhould fay you hold your Land by *Mofes*
or Gods Law, and would try it by that, you may perhaps loofe, but by the Law of the Kingdom you are
fure of it, fo may the Bifhops by this Plea of *Jure
Divino* loofe all; The Pope had as good a Title by
the Law of *England* as could be had, had he not left
that, and claim'd by Power from God.

7. There is no Government enjoyn'd by Example,
but by Precept; it does not follow we muft have
Bifhops ftill, becaufe we have had them fo long. They
are equally mad who fay Bifhops are fo *Jure Divino*
that they muft be continued, and they who fay
are fo Antichriftian, that they muft be put away,
as the State pleafes.

8. To have no Minifters, but Presbyters, 'tis as in
the Temporal ftate they fhould have no Officers but
Conftables. Bifhops do beft ftand with Monarchy,
thus as amongft the Laity, you have Dukes, Lords,
Lieutenants, Judges, &c. to fend down the Kings
pleafure to his Subjects; So you have Bifhops to
govern the inferiour Clergy: Thefe upon occafion may
addrefs themfelves to the King, otherwife every Parfon
of the Parifh muft come, and run up to the Court.

9. The Proteſtants have no Biſhops in *France*, becauſe they live in a Catholic Country, and they will not have Catholic Biſhops; therefore they muſt govern themſelves as well as they may.

10. What is that to the purpoſe, to what end Biſhops Lands were given to them at firſt? you muſt look to the Law and Cuſtom of the place. What is that to any Temporal Lords Eſtate, how Lands were firſt divided, or how in *William* the Conquerours days? And if Men at firſt were juggled out of their Eſtates, yet they are rightly their Succeſſours. If my Father cheat a Man, and he conſent to it, the Inheritance is rightly mine.

11. If there be no Biſhops, there muſt be something elſe, which has the Power of Biſhops, though it be in many, and then had you not as good keep them? If you will have no Half Crowns, but only ſingle Pence, yet Thirty ſingle Pence are a Half-Crown; and then had you not as good keep both? But the Biſhops have done ill, 'twas the Men, not the Function; As if you ſhould ſay, you would have no more Half Crowns, becauſe they were ſtolen, when the truth is they were not ſtolen becauſe they were Half-Crowns, but becauſe they were Money and light in a Thieves hand.

12. They that would pull down the Biſhops and erect a new way of Government, do as he that pulls down an old Houſe, and builds another, in another faſhion, there's a great deal of do, and a great deal of trouble, the old rubbiſh muſt be carryed away, and new materials muſt be brought, Workmen muſt be provided, and perhaps the old one would have ſerv'd as well.

13. If the Parliament and *Presbyterian Party* ſhould diſpute who ſhould be Judge? Indeed in the beginning of Queen *Elizabeth*, there was ſuch a difference, between the *Proteſtants* and *Papiſts*, and Sir *Nicholas Bacon* Lord Chancellor was appointed to be Judge, but the Concluſion was the ſtronger *Party* carryed it: For ſo Religion was brought into Kingdoms, ſo it has

been continued, and fo it may be caft out, when the State pleafes.

14. 'Twill be a great difcouragement to Scholars that *Bifhops* fhould be put down: For now the Father can fay to his Son, and the Tutor to his *Pupil, Study hard, and you fhall have Vocem et Sedem in Parliamento*; then it muft be, *Study hard, and you fhall have a hundred a year if you pleafe your Parifh*. *Obj*. But they that enter into the Miniftry for preferment, are like *Judas* that lookt after the *Bag*. *Anf*. It may be fo, if they turn Scholars at *Judas's* Age, but what Arguments will they ufe to perfwade them to follow their *Books* while they are young?

Books, Authors.

1. THE giving a *Bookfeller* his price for his *Books* has this advantage, he that will do fo, fhall have the refufal of whatfoever comes to his hand, and fo by that means get many things, which otherwife he never fhould have feen. So 'tis in giving a *Bawd* her price.

2. In buying Books or other Commodities, 'tis not always the beft way to bid half fo much as the feller asks: witnefs the Country fellow that went to buy two groat Shillings, they askt him three Shillings, and he bid them Eighteen Pence.

3. They counted the price of the Books (*Acts* 19. 19.) and found Fifty Thoufand pieces of Silver, that is fo many Sextertii, or fo many three half pence of our Money, about Three Hundred pound Sterling.

4. Popifh Books teach and inform, what we know, we know much out of them. The Fathers, Church Story, Schoolmen, all may pafs for Popifh Books, and if you take away them, what Learning will you leave? Befides who muft be Judge? The Cuftomer or the Waiter? If he difallows a Book it muft not be brought into the Kingdom, then Lord have mercy upon all Schollars. Thefe Puritan Preachers if they have any things good, they have it out of Popifh Books, though they will not acknowledg[e] it, for fear of difpleafing

the people, he is a poor Divine that cannot sever the good from the bad.

5. 'Tis good to have Translations, because they serve as a Comment, so far as the Judgement of the Man goes.

6. In Answering a Book, 'tis best to be short, otherwise he that I write against will suspect I intend to weary him, not to satisfy him Besides in being long I shall give my Adversary a huge advantage, somewhere or other he will pick a hole.

7. In quoting of Books, quote such Authors as are usually read, others you may read for your own Satisfaction, but not name them.

8. Quoting of Authors is most for matter of Fact, and then I write them as I would produce a Witness, sometimes for a free Expression, and then I give the Author his due, and gain my self praise by reading him.

9. To quote a modern *Dutch* Man where I may use a Classic Author, is as if I were to justify my Reputation, and I neglect all Persons of Note and Quality that know me, and bring the Testimonial of the Scullion in the Kitchen.

Cannon Laws.

IF I would study the Cannon-Law as it is used in *England*, I must study the Heads here in use, then go to the Practicers in those Courts where that Law is practised, and know their Customs, so for all the study in the World.

Ceremony.

1. Ceremony keeps up all things; 'Tis like a Penny-Glass to a rich Spirit, or some Excellent Water, without it the water were spilt, the Spirit lost.

2. Of all people Ladies have no reason to cry down Ceremonies, for they take themselves slighted without it. And were they not used with Ceremony, with Complements and Addresses, with Legs, and Kissing of Hands, they were the pittyfullest Creatures in the World, but yet methinks to kiss their Hands after their

Lips as some do, is like little Boys, that after they eat the Apple, fall to the paring, out of a Love they have to the Apple.

Chancellor.

1. THE Bishop is not to fit with the Chancellor in his Court (as being a thing either beneath him, or befide him) no more then the King is to fit in the *Kings-Bench* when he has made a Lord-Chief-Juftice.

2. The Chancellor govern'd in the Church, a Layman. And therefore 'tis falfe which the the Bifhops with, that they Challenge fole Jurifdiction. For the Bifhop can no more put out the Chancellor than the Chancellor the Bifhop. They were many of them made Chancellors for their Lives, and he is the fitteft Man to Govern, becaufe Divinity fo o the reft.

Changing Sides.

1. 'TIS the Tryal of a Man to fee if he will Change his fide, and if he be fo weak as to Change once, he will Change again. Your Country Fellows have a way to try if a Man be weak in the Hams, by coming behind him, and giving him a blow unawares, if he bend once, he will bend again.

2. The Lords that fall from the King after they have got Eftates, by bafe Flattery at Court, and now pretend Confcience, do as a Vintner, that when he firft fets up, you may bring your Wench to his Houfe, and do your things there, but when he grows Rich, he turns Confcientious, and will fell no Wine upon the Sabbath-day.

3. Collonel *Goring* ferving firft the one fide and then the other, did like a good Miller that knows how to grind which way foever the Wind fits.

4. After *Luther* had made a Combuftion in *Germany* about Religion, he was fent to by the *Pope*, to be taken off, and offer'd any preferment in the Church, that he would make choice of, *Luther* anfwer'd, if he had offered half as much at firft, he would have accepted

it, but now he had gone so far, he could not come back, in Truth he had made himself a greater thing than they could make him, the *German* Princes Courted him, he was become the Authour of a Sect ever after to be called *Lutherans*. So have our Preachers done that are against the Bishops, they have made themselves greater with the People, than they can be made the other way, and therefore there is the less Charity probably in bringing them of. Charity to Strangers is injoyned in the Text, by Strangers is there understood those that are not of our own kin, Strangers to your Blood, not those who cannot tell whence they came, that is be Charitable to your Neighbours whom you know to be honest poor People.

Christmas.

1. CHristmas succeeds the *Saturnalia*, the same time, the same number of Holy days, then the Master waited upon the Servant like the Lord of *Misrule*.

2. Our Meats and our Sports (much of them) have relation to Church-works. The Coffin of our *Christmas* Pies in shape long, is in imitation of the Cratch, our Choosing Kings and Queens on Twelfth night, hath reference to the Three Kings. So likewise our eating of Fritters, whipping of Tops, Roasting of Herrings, Jack of Lents, &c. they were all in imitation of Church-works, Emblems of *Martyrdom*. Our Tansies at *Easter* have reference to the bitter Herbs: though at the same time 'twas always the Fashion for a Man to have a Gammon of Bakon, to show himself to be no *Jew*.

Christians.

1. IN the High Church of *Jerusalem*, the Christians were but another Sect of *Jews*, that did believe the *Messias* was come. To be called was nothing else, but to become a Christian, to have the Name of a Christian, it being their own Language, for amongst the *Jews*, when they made a Doctor of Law, *hammasaid* he was called.

2. The *Turks* tell their People of a Heaven where there is fenfible Pleafure, but of a Hell where they fhall fuffer they do not know what. The Chriftians quite invert this order, they tell us of a Hell where we fhall feel fenfible Pain, but of a Heaven where we fhall enjoy we cannot tell what.

3. Why did the Heathens object to the Chriftians, that they Worfhip an Affes Head? you muft know, that to a Heathen, a *Jew* and a Chriftian were all one, that they regarded him not, fo he was not one of them. Now that of the Affes Head might proceed from fuch a miftake as this, by the *Jews* Law all the Firftlings of Cattle were to be offered to God, except a Young Afs, which was to be redeem'd, a Heathen being prefent, and feeing young Calves, and young Lambs killed at their Sacrifices, only young Affes redeem'd might very well think they had that filly Beaft in fome high Eftimation, and thence might imagine they worfhipt it as a God.

Church.

1. HEretofore the Kingdom let the Church alone, let them do what they would, becaufe they had fomething elfe to think of (*viz.*) Wars, but now in time of peace, we begin to examine all things, will have nothing but what we like, grow dainty and wanton, juft as in a Family the Heir ufes to go a hunting, he never confiders how his Meal is dreft, takes a bit, and away, but when he ftays within, then he grows curious, he does not like this, nor he does not like that, he will have his Meat dreft his own way, or peradventure he will drefs it himfelf.

2. It hath ever been the gain of the Church when the King will let the Church have no Power to cry down the King and cry up the Church: but when the Church can make ufe of the Kings Power, then to bring all under the Kings Perogative, the Catholicks of *England* go one way, and the Court Clergy another.

3. A glorious Church is like a Magnificent Feaft there is all the variety that may be, but every one

choofes out a difh or two that he likes, and lets the reft alone, how Glorious foever the Church is, every one choofes out of it his own Religion, by which he governs himfelf and lets the reft alone.

4. The Laws of the Church are moft Favourable to the Church, becaufe they were the Churches own making, as the Heralds are the beft Gentlemen becaufe they make their own Pedigree.

5. There is a Queftion about that Article, Concerning the Power of the Church, whether thefe words [of having Power in Controverfies of Faith] were not ftoln in, but 'tis moft certain they were in the Book of Articles that was Confirm'd, though in fome Editions they have been left out: But the Article before tells you, who the Church is, not the Clergy, but *Cætus fidelium*.

Church of Rome.

1. BEfore a Juglars Tricks are difcovered we admire him, and give him Money, but afterwards we care not for them, fo 'twas before the difcovery of the Jugling of the Church of *Rome*.

2. Catholics fay, we out of our Charity, believe they of the Church of *Rome* may be faved: But they do not believe fo of us. Therefore their Church is better according to our felves; firft, fome of them no doubt believe as well of us, as we do of them, but they muft not fay fo, befides is that an Argument their Church is better than Ours, becaufe it has lefs Charity?

3. One of the *Church* of *Rome* will not come to our Prayers, does that agree he doth not like them? I would fain fee a *Catholic* leave his Dinner, becaufe a Nobleman's *Chaplain* fays Grace, nor haply would he leave the Prayers of the *Church*, if going to *Church* were not made a mark of diftinction between a *Proteftant* and a *Papift*.

Churches.

1. THE Way coming into our great Churches was Antiently at the Weft door, that Men might fee the Altar, and all the Church before them, the other Doors were but Pofterns.

City.

1. WHat makes a City? Whether a Bishoprick or any of that nature? *Anfwer.* 'Tis according to the firft Charter which made them a Corporation. If they are Incorporated by Name of *Civitas* they are a City, if by the name of *Burgum*, then they are a Burrough.

2. The Lord Mayor of *London* by their firft Charter was to be prefented to the King, in his abfence to the Lord Chief Jufticiary of *England*, afterwards to the Lord Chancellor, now to the Barons of the Exchequer, but ftill there was a Refervation, that for their Honour they fhould come once a Year to the King, as they do ftill.

Clergy.

1. THough a Clergy-Man have no Faults of his own, yet the Faults of the whole Tribe fhall be laid upon him, fo that he fhall be fure not to lack.

2. The Clergy would have us believe them againft our own Reafon, as the Woman would have her Husband againft his own Eyes: What! will you believe your own Eyes before your own fweet Wife?

3. The Condition of the Clergy towards their Prince, and the Condition of the Phyfitian is all one: the Phyfitians tell the Prince they have Agrick and Rubarb, good for him, and good for his Subjects bodies, upon this he gives them leave to ufe it, but if it prove naught, then away with it, they fhall ufe it no more. So the Clergy tell the Prince they have Phyfick good for his Soul, and good for the Souls of his People, upon that he admits them: but when he finds by Experience they both trouble him and his People, he will have no more to do with them, what is that to them or any body elfe if a King will not go to Heaven.

4. A Clergy Man goes not a dram further than this, you ought to obey your Prince in general (if he does he is loft] how to obey him you muft be inform'd by thofe whofe profeffion it is to tell you. The Parfon

of the Tower (a good difcreet Man) told Dr. *Mofely* (who was fent to me, and the reft of the Gentlemen Committed the 3. *Caroli*, to perfwade Us to fubmit to the King) that they found no fuch words as [Parliament, *Habeas Corpus*, *Return*, *Tower*, &c.] Neither in the Fathers, nor the School-Men, nor in the Text, and therefore for his part he believed he underftood nothing of the bufinefs. A Satyr upon all thofe Clergy Men that meddle with·Matters they do not underftand.

All Confefs there never was a more Learned Clergy, no Man taxes them with Ignorance. But to talk of that, is like the Fellow that was a great Wentcher he wifht God would forgive him his Leachery, and lay Ufury to his Charge. The Clergy have worfe Faults.

6. The Clergy and Laity together are never like to do well, 'tis as if a Man were to make an Excellent Feaft and fhould have his Apothecary and Phyfitian come into the Kitchen : The Cooks if they were let alone would make Excellent Meat, but then comes the Apothecary and he puts Rubarb into one Sauce, and Agrick into another Sauce. Chain up the Clergy on both fides.

High Commission.

1. MEN cry out upon the High-Commiffion, as if the Clergy-men only had to do in it, when I believe there are more Lay-men in Commiffion there, than Clergymen, if the Laymen will not come, whofe fault is that? So of the Star-Chamber the People think the Bifhops only cenfur'd *Prin*, *Burton* and *Baftwick*, when there were but two there, and one speak not in his own Caufe.

House of Commons.

2. THere be but two Erroneous Opinions in the Houfe of Commons, That the Lords fit only for themfelves, when the truth is, they fit as well for the Common-wealth. The Knights and Burgeffes fit for themfelves and others, fome for more, fome for fewer, and what is the reafon ? Becaufe the Room will not hold all, the Lords being

few, they all come, and imagine a Room able to hold all the Commons of *England*, then the Lords and Burgeſſes would ſit no otherwiſe than the Lords do. The ſecond Error is, that the Houſe of Commons are to begin to give Subſidies, yet if the Lords diſſent they can give no Money.

2. The Houſe of Commons is called the Lower Houſe in Twenty Acts of Parliament, but what are Twenty Acts of Parliament amongſt Friends?

3. The Form of a Charge runs thus, *I Accuſe in the Name of all the Commons of* England, how then can any man be as a Witneſs, when every man is made the Accuſer?

Confeſſion.

1. IN time of Parliament it uſed to be one of the firſt things the Houſe did, to petition the King that his Confeſſor might be removed, as fearing either his power with the King, or elſe, leaſt he ſhould reveal to the Pope what the Houſe was in doing, as no doubt he did, when the Catholick Cauſe was concerned.

2. The difference between us and the *Papiſts* is, we both allow Contrition, but the *Papiſts* make Confeſſion a part of Contrition, they ſay a Man is not ſufficiently contrite, till he confeſs his ſins to a Prieſt.

3. Why ſhould I think a Prieſt will not reveal Confeſſion, I am ſure he will do anything that is forbidden him, haply not ſo often as I, the utmoſt puniſhment is Deprivation, and how can it be proved, that ever any man reveal'd Confeſſion, when there is no Witneſs? And no man can be Witneſs in his own cauſe. A meer Gullery. There was a time when 'twas publick in the Church, and there is much againſt their Auricular Confeſſion.

Competency.

1. THat which is a Competency for one Man, is not enough for another, no more than that which will keep one Man warm, will keep another Man warm; one man can go in Doublet and

Hofe, when another Man cannot be without a Cloak, and yet have no more Cloaths than is neceffary for him.

Great-Conjunction.

THE greateft Conjunction of *Saturn* and *Jupiter*, happens but once in Eight Hundred Years, and therefore Aftrologers can make no Experiments of it, nor foretel what it means, (not but what the Stars may mean fomthing, but we cannot tell what) becaufe we cannot come at them. Suppofe a Planet were a Simple, or an Herb, How could a Phyfician tell the Vertue of that Simple, unlefs he could come at it, to apply it?

Conscience.

1. HE that hath a Scrupulous Confcience, is like a Horfe that is not well weigh'd, he ftarts at every Bird that flies out of the Hedge.

2. A Knowing Man will do that, which a tender Confcience Man dares not do, by reafon of his Ignorance, the other knows there is no hurt, as a Child is afraid to go into the dark, when a Man is not, becaufe he knows there is no danger.

3. If we once come to leave that out-loofe, as to pretend Confcience againft Law, who knows what inconvenience may follow? For thus, Suppofe an *Anabaptift* comes and takes my Horfe, I Sue him, he tells me he did according to his Confcience, his Confcience tells him all things are common amongft the Saints, what is mine is his, therefore you do ill to make fuch a Law, If any Man takes anothers Horfe he fhall be hang'd. What can I fay to this Man? He does according to his Confcience. Why is not he as honeft a Man as he that pretends a Ceremony eftablifht by Law, is againft his Confcience? Generally to pretend Confcience againft Law is dangerous, in fome cafes haply we may.

4. Some men make it a cafe of Confcience, whether a man may have a Pidgeon-houfe, becaufe his Pidgeons eat other Folks Corn. But there is no fuch thing as

Confcience in the bufinefs, the matter is,
be a man of fuch Quality,
to have a Dove-houfe, if fo there's an end
nefs, his Pidgeons have a right to eat where
pleafe themfelves.

Confecrated Places.

1. THE *Jews* had a peculiar way of Confecrating things to God, which we have not.

2. Under the Law, God, who was Mafter of all, made choice of a Temple to Worfhip in, where he was more efpecially prefent: Juft as the Mafter of the Houfe, who ow[n]s all the Houfe, makes choice of one Chamber to lie in, which is called the Mafter's Chamber, but under the Gofpel there was no fuch thing, Temples and Churches are fet apart for the conveniency of men to Worfhip in; they cannot meet upon the point of a Needle, but God himfelf makes no choice.

3. All things are Gods already, we can give him no right by confecrating any, that he had not before, only we fet it apart to his Service. Juft as a Gardiner brings his Lord and Mafter a Basket of Apricocks, and prefents them, his Lord thanks him, perhaps gives him fomething for his pains, and yet the Apricocks were as much his Lords before as now.

4. What is Confecrated, is given to fome particular man, to do God Service, not given to God, but given to Man, to ferve God: And there's not any thing, Lands or Goods, but fome men or other have it in their power, to difpofe of as they pleafe. The faying things Confecrated cannot be taken away, makes men afraid of Confecration.

5. Yet Confecration has this Power, when a Man has Confecrated any thing to God, he cannot of himfelf take it away.

Contracts.

1. F our Fathers have loft their Liberty, why may not we labour to regain it? *Anfw.* We muft look to the Contract, if that be rightly made we muft ftand to it, if we once grant we may recede

from Contracts upon any inconveniency that may afterwards happen, we shall have no Bargain kept. If I sell you a Horse, and do not like my Bargain, I will have my Horse again.

2. Keep your Contracts, so far a Divine goes, but how to make our Contracts is left to our selves, and as we agree upon the conveying of this House, or that Land, so it must be, if you offer me a hundred pounds for my Glove. I tell you what my Glove is, a plain Glove, pretend no virtue in it, the Glove is my own, I profess not to sell Gloves, and we agree for an hundred pounds. I do not know why I may not with a safe Conscience take it. The want of that common Obvious Distinction of *Jus præceptivum*, and *Jus permissum*, does much trouble men.

3. Lady *Kent* Articled with Sir *Edward Herbert*, that he should come to her when she sent for him, and stay with her as long as she would have him, to which he set his hand; then he Articled with her, That he should go away when he pleas'd, and stay away as long as he pleas'd, to which she set her hand. This is the Epitome of all the Contracts in the World, betwixt man and man, betwixt Prince and Subject, they keep them as long as they like them, and no longer.

Council.

1. They talk (but blasphemously enough) that the Holy Ghost is President of their General-Councils, when the truth is, the odd man is still the Holy-Obost.

Convocation.

1. When the King sends his Writ for a Parliament, he sends for two Knights for a Shire, and two Burgesses for a Corporation: But when he sends for two Archbishops for a Convocation, he commands them to assemble the whole Clergy, but they out of custome amongst themselves send to the Bishops of their Provinces to will them to bring two Clarks for a Diocese, the Dean, one

for the Chapter, and the Arch-deacons, but to the King every Clergy-man is there prefent.

2. We have nothing fo nearly expreffes the power of a Convocation, in refpect of a Parliament, as a Court-Leet, where they have a power to make By-Laws, as they call them; as that a man fhall put fo many Cows, or fheep in the Common, but they can make nothing that is contrary to the Laws of the Kingdom.

Creed.

1. A *Thanafius's* Creed is the fhorteft, take away the Preface, and the force, and the Conclufion, which are not part of the Creed. In the *Nicene* Creed it is εἰς ἐκκλησίαν, I believe in the Church, but now, as our Common-prayer has it, I believe one Catholick and Apoftolick Church; they like not Creeds, becaufe they would have no Forms of Faith, as they have none of Prayer, though there be more reafon for the one than for the other.

Damnation.

1. IF the Phyfician fees you eat anything that is not good for your Body, to keep you from it, he crys 'tis poyfon, if the Divine fees you do any thing that is hurtful for your Soul, to keep you from it, he crys out you are damn'd.

2. To preach long, loud, and Damnation is the way to be cry'd up. We love a man that Damns us, and we run after him again to fave us. If a man had a fore Leg, and he fhould go to an Honeft Judicious Chyrurgeon, and he fhould only bid him keep it warm, and anoint with fuch an Oyl (an Oyl well known) that would do the Cure, haply he would not much regard him, becaufe he knows the Medecine before hand an ordinary Medecine. But if he fhould go to a Surgeon that fhould tell him your Leg will Gangreen within three days, and it muft be cut off, and you will die, unlefs you do fomething that I could tell you, what liftning there would be to this Man? Oh for the Lord's fake, tell me what this is, I will give you any content for your pains.

Devils.

1. WHY have we none poffeft with Devils in England? The old Anfwer is, the Proteftants the Devil hath already, and the Papifts are fo Holy, he dares not meddle with them. Why, then beyond Seas where a Nun is poffeft, when a *Hugonot* comes into the Church, does not the Devil hunt them out? The Prieft teaches him, you never faw the Devil throw up a Nuns Coats, mark that, the Prieft will not fuffer it, for then the People will fpit at him.

2. Cafting out Devils is meer Juggling, they never caft out any but what they firft caft in. They do it where for Reverence no man fhall dare to Examine it, they do it in a Corner, in a Mortice-hole, not in the Market-place. They do nothing but what may be done by Art, they make the Devil fly out of the Window in the likenefs of a Bat, or a Rat, why do they not hold him? Why, in the likenefs of a Bat, or a Rat, or fome Creature? That is why not in fome fhape we Paint him in, with Claws and Horns? By this trick they gain much, gain upon Mens fancies, and fo are reverenc'd, and certainly if the Prieft deliver me from him, that is my moft deadly Enemy, I have all the Reafon in the World to Reverence him. Objection. But if this be Juggling, why do they punifh Impoftures? *Anfwer*. For great Reafon, becaufe they do not play their part well, and for fear others fhould difcover them, and fo all of them ought to be of the fame Trade.

3. A Perfon of Quality came to my Chamber in the Temple, and told me he had two Devils in his head [I wonder'd what he meant] and juft at that time, one of them bid him kill me, [with that I begun to be afraid and thought he was mad] he faid he knew I could Cure him, and therefore intreated me to give him fomething, for he was refolv'd to go to no body elfe. I perceiving what an Opinion he had of me, and that 'twas only Melancholy that troubl'd him, took him in

hand, warranted him, if he would follow my directions, to Cure him in a short time. I defired him to let me be alone about an hour, and then to come again, which he was very willing to. In the mean time I got a Card, and lapt it up handfome in a piece of Taffata, and put ftrings to the Taffata, and when he came gave it to him, to hang about his Neck, withal charged him, that he fhould not diforder himfelf neither with eating or drinking, but eat very little of Supper, and fay his Prayers duly when he went to Bed, and I made no queftion but he would be well in three or four days. Within that time I went to Dinner to his Houfe and askt him how he did? He faid he was much better, but not perfectly well, or in truth he had not dealt clearly with me, he had four Devils in his head, and he perceiv'd two of them were gone, with that which I had given him, but the other two troubled him ftill. Well faid I, I am glad two of them are gone I make no doubt but to get away the other two likewife. So I gave him another thing to hang about his Neck, three days after he came to me to my Chamber and profeft he was now as well as ever he was in his life, and did extreamly thank me for the great care I had taken of him, I fearing leaft he might relapfe into the like Diftemper, told him that there was none but my felf, and one Phyfitian more in the whole Town that could Cure the Devils in the head, and that was Dr. *Harvey* (whom I had prepar'd) and wifht him if ever he found himfelf ill in my abfence to go to him, for he could Cure his Difeafe, as well as my felf. The Gentleman lived many Years and was never troubl'd after.

Self Denyal.

1. 'TIS much the Doctrine of the times that Men fhould not pleafe themfelves, but deny themfelves every thing they take delight in, not look upon Beauty, wear no good Clothes, eat no good Meat, &c. which feems the greateft Accufation that can be upon the maker of all good things. If

they be not to be us'd, why did God make them? The truth is, they that preach againſt them, cannot make uſe of them their ſelves, and then again they get Eſteem by ſeeming to contemn them. But mark it while you live, if they do not pleaſe themſelves as much as they can, and we live more by Example than precept.

Duell.

1. A Duell may ſtill be granted in ſome Caſes by the Law of *England*, and only there. That the Church allow'd it Antiently, appears by this, in their publick Liturgies there were Prayers appointed for the Duelifts to ſay, the Judge, uſed to bid them go to ſuch a Church and pray, &c. But whether is this Lawful? If you grant any War Lawful, I make no doubt but to Convince it, War is Lawful, becauſe God is the only Judge between two, that is Supream. Now if a difference happen between two Subjects, and it cannot be decided by Human Teſtimony, why may they not put it to God to Judge between them by the Permiſſion of the Prince? Nay what if we ſhould bring it down for Arguments ſake, to the Swordmen. One gives me the Lye, 'tis a great diſgrace to take it, the Law has made no proviſion to give Remedy for the Injury (if you can ſuppoſe any thing an Injury for which the Law gives no Remedy) why am not I in this caſe Supream, and may therefore right my ſelf.

2. A Duke ought to fight with a Gentleman, the Reaſon is this, the Gentleman will ſay to the Duke 'tis True, you hold a higher Place in the State than I, there's a great diſtance between you and me, but your Dignity does not Priviledge you to do me an Injury, as ſoon as ever you do me an Injury, you make your ſelf my equal, and as you are my equal I Challenge you, and in fence the Duke is bound to Anſwer him. This will give you ſome light to vnderſtand the Quarrel betwixt a Prince and his Subjects, though there be a vaſt diſtance between him and them, and they are to obey him, according to their Contract, yet he hath

no power to do them an Injury, then they think themselves as much bound to Vindicate their right, as they are to obey his Lawful Commands, nor is there any other meafure of Juftice left upon Earth but Arms.

Epitaph.

AN *Epitaph* muft be made fit for the Perfon for whom it is made, for a Man to fay all the Excellent things, that can be faid upon one, and call that his *Epitaph*, is as if a Painter fhould make the handfomeft piece he can poffibly make, and fay 'twas my Picture. It holds in a Funeral Sermon.

Equity.

1. EQuity in Law is the fame that the Spirit is in Religion, what every one pleafes to make it, fometimes they go according to Confcience, fometimes according to Law, fometimes according to the Rule of Court.

2. Equity is a Roguifh thing, for Law we have a meafure, know what to truft to, Equity is according to Confcience of him that is Chancellor, and as that is larger or narrower, fo is Equity. 'Tis all one as if they fhould make the Standard for the meafure, we call a Chancellors Foot, what an uncertain meafure would this be? One Chancellor has a long Foot, another a fhort Foot, a third an indifferent Foot. 'Tis the fame thing in the Chancellors Confcience.

3. That faying, do as you would be done to, is often mifunderftood, for 'tis not thus meant that I a Man, fhould do to you a private Man, as I would have you to me, but do, as we have agreed to do one to another by publick Agreement, If the Prifoner fhould ask the Judge, whether he would be content to be hang'd, were he in his Cafe, he would anfwer no. Then fays the Prifoner, do as you would be done to; neither of them muft do as private Men, but the Judge muft do by him as they have publickly agreed, that is both Judge and Prifoner have confented to a Law that if either of them Steal, they fhall be hanged.

Evil-Speaking.

1. HE that fpeaks ill of another commonly before he is aware, makes himfelf fuch a one as he fpeaks againft, for if he had the Civility or breeding he would forbear fuch kind of Language.

2. A Gallant Man is above ill words: an Example we have in the old Lord of *Salisbury* (who was a great wife Man) *Stone* had call'd fome Lord about Court, Fool, the Lord complains and has *Stone* whipt, *Stone* cries, I might have called my Lord of *Salisbury* Fool often enough, before he would have had me whipt.

3. Speak not ill of a great Enemy but rather give him good words, that he may ufe you the better, if you chance to fall into his Hands, the Spaniard did this when he was dying, his Confeffor told him (to work him to Repentance) how the Devil Tormented the wicked that went to Hell: the *Spaniard* replying, called the Devil my Lord. I hope my Lord the Devil is not fo Cruel, his Confeffor reproved him. Excufe me faid the *Don*, for calling him fo, I know not into what hands I may fall, and if I happen into his, I hope he will ufe me the better for giving him good words.

Excommunication.

1. THat place they bring for Excommunication [put away from among your felves that wicked person, 1 *Cor.* 5. *Cha:* 13. *verfe*] is corrupted in the *Greek*. for it fhould be τὸ πονηρὸν, put away that Evil from among you, not τὸν πονηρὸν, that Evil Perfon, befides ὁ πονηρὸς is the Devil in Scripture, and it may be so taken there, and there is a new Edition of *Theoderet* come out, that has its right τὸ πονηρὸν. 'Tis true the Chriftians before the Civil State became Chriftian, did by Covenant and Agreement fet down how they fhould live; and he that did not obferve what they agreed upon, fhould come no more amongft them, that is, be Excommunicated. Such Men are fpoken of by the *Apoftle* [*Romans* 1. 31.] who he

calls ἀσωθέτοις καὶ ἀσωόνδοις, the Vulgar has it, *Incompofit, et fine fœdre,* the laſt word is pretty well, but the firſt not at all, *Origen* in his Book againſt *Celfus*, ſpeaks of the Chriſtians. συθείκη: the Tranſlation renders it *Conventus,* as it ſignifies a Meeting, when it is plain it ſignifies a Covenant, and the *Engliſh* Bible turned the other word well, Covenant-breakers. *Pliny* tells us, the Chriſtians took an Oath amongſt themſelves to live thus, and thus.

2. The other place [*Dic Ecclefiæ*] tell the Church, is but a weak Ground to raiſe Excommunication upon, eſpecially from the Sacrament, the leſſer Excommunication, ſince when that was ſpoken, the Sacrament was inſtituted. The *Jews Ecclefia* was their *Sanhedrim*, their Court: ſo that the meaning is: if after once or twice *Admonition* this Brother will not be reclaim'd, bring him thither.

3. The firſt Excommunication was 180. Years after Chriſt, and that by Victor, Biſhop of *Rome.* But that was no more than this, that they ſhould Communicate and receive the Sacrament amongſt themſelves, not with thoſe of the other Opinion: The Controverſie (as I take it) being about the Feaſt of *Eaſter.* Men do not care for Excommunication becauſe they are ſhut out of the Church, or delivered up to *Sathan,* but becauſe the Law of the Kingdom takes hold of them, after ſo many days a Man cannot Sue, no, not for his Wife, if you take her from him, and there may be as much Reaſon, to grant it for a ſmall Fault, if there be Contumacy, as for a great one, in *Weſtminſter-Hall* you you may Out-law a Man for forty Shillings, which is their Excommunication, and you can do no more for forty Thouſand Pound.

4. When *Conſtantine* became Chriſtian, he ſo fell in love with the Clergy, that he let them be Judges of all things, but that continued not above three or four Years, by reaſon they were to be Judges of matters they underſtood not, and then they were allowed to meddle with nothing but Religion, all Juriſdiction belonged to him, and he ſcanted them out as much as

be pleafed, and fo things have fince continued. They Excommunicate for three or four things, matters concerning Adultery, Tythes, Wills, &c. which is the Civil Punifhment the State allows for fuch Faults. If a Bifhop Excommunicate a Man for what he ought not, the Judge has Power to abfolve, and punifh the Bifhop, if they had that Jurifdiction from God, why does not the Church Excommunicate for Murder, for Theft? If the Civil Power 'might take away all but three things, why may they not take them away to? If this Excommunication were taken away, the Presbyters would be quiet; 'tis that they have a mind to, 'tis that they would fain be at, like the Wench that was to be Married; fhe asked her Mother when 'twas done, if fhe fhould go to Bed prefently: no fays her Mother you muft Dine firft, and then to Bed Mother? no you muft Dance after Dinner, and then to Bed Mother, no you muft go to Supper, and then to Bed Mother, &c.

Faith and Works.

1. 'TWas an unhappy Divifion that has been made between Faith and Works; though in my Intellect I may divide them, juft as in the Candle, I know there is both light and heat. But yet put out the Candle, and they are both gone, one remains not without the other: So 'tis betwixt Faith and Works; nay, in a right Conception *Fides eft opus*, if I believe a thing becaufe I am commanded, that is *Opus*.

Fasting-days.

1. WHat the Church debars us one day, fhe gives us leave to take out in another. Firft we Faft, and then we Feaft; firft there is a Carnival, and then a Lent.

2. Whether do Human Laws bind the Confcience? If they do, 'tis a way to enfnare: If we fay they do not, we open the door to difobedience. *Anfw*. In this Cafe we muft look to the Juftice of the Law, and intention of the Law-giver. If there be no Juftice in

the Law, 'tis not to be obey'd, if the intention of the Law-giver be abfolute, our obedience muft be fo too. If the intention of the Law-giver enjoyn a Penalty as a Compenfation for the Breach of the Law, I fin not, if I fubmit to the Penalty, if it enjoyn a Penalty, as a further enforcement of Obedience to the Law, then ought I to obferve it, which may be known by the often repetition of the Law. The way of Fafting is enjoyn'd unto them, who yet do not obferve it. The Law enjoyns a Penalty as an enforcement to Obedience; which intention appears by the often calling upon us, to keep that Law by the King and the Difpenfation of the Church to fuch as are not able to keep it, as Young Children, Old Folks, Disfeas'd Men, &c.

Fathers and Sons.

1. IT hath ever been the way for Fathers, to bind their Sons, to ftrengthen this by the Law of the Land, every one at Twelve Years of age, is to take the Oath of Allegiance in Court-Leets, whereby he fwears Obedience to the King.

Fines.

1. THE old Law was, That when a Man was Fin'd, he was to be Fin'd *Salvo Contenemento*, fo as his Countenance might be fafe, taking Countenance in the fame fenfe as your Countryman does, when he fays, if you will come unto my Houfe, I will fhow you the beft Countenance I can, that is not the beft Face, but the beft Entertainment. The meaning of the Law was, that fo much fhould be taken from a man, fuch a Gobbet fliced off, that yet notwithftanding he might live in the fame Rank and Condition he lived in before; but now they Fine men ten times more than they are worth.

Free-will.

1. THE *Puritans* who will allow no free-will at all, but God does all, yet will allow the Subject his Liberty to do, or not to do, notwithftanding the King, the God upon Earth. The

Arminians, who hold we have free-will, yet fay, when we come to the King, there muſt be all Obedience, and no Liberty to be ſtood for.

Fryers.

1. THE Fryers ſay they poſſeſs nothing, whoſe then are the Lands they hold? not their Superiour's, he hath vow'd Poverty as well as they, whoſe then? To anſwer this, 'twas Decreed they ſhould ſay they were the Popes. And why muſt the Fryers be more perfect than the Pope himſelf?

2. If there had been no Fryers, *Chriſtendome* might have continu'd quiet, and things remain'd at a ſtay.

If there had been no Lecturers (which ſucceed the Friers in their way) the Church of *England* might have ſtood, and flouriſht at this day.

Friends.

1. OLD Friends are heſt. King *James* us'd to call for his Old Shoos, they were eaſieſt for his Feet.

Genealogy of Chriſt.

1. THey that ſay the reaſon why *Joſeph*'s Pedigree is ſet down, and not *Mary*'s, is, becauſe the deſcent from the Mother is loſt, and ſwallow'd up, ſay ſomething; but yet if a *Jewiſh* Woman, marry'd a *Gentil*, they only took notice of the Mother, not of the Father; but they that ſay they were both of a Tribe, ſay nothing, for the Tribes might Marry one with another, and the Law againſt it was only Temporary, in the time while *Joſhua* was dividing the Land, leaſt the being ſo long about it, there might be a confuſion.

2. That Chriſt was the Son of *Joſeph* is moſt exactly true. For though he was the Son of God, yet with the *Jews*, if any man kept a Child, and brought him up, and call'd him Son, he was taken for his Son; and his Land (if he had any) was to deſcend upon him; and therefore the Genealogy of *Joſeph* is juſtly ſet down.

Gentlemen.

1. WHat a Gentleman is, 'tis hard with us to define, in other Countries he is known by his Privileges; in *Westminster* Hall he is one that is reputed one; in the Court of Honour, he that hath Arms. The King cannot make a Gentleman of Blood [what have you said] nor God Almighty, but he can make a Gentleman by Creation. If you ask which is the better of these two, Civilly, the Gentleman of Blood, Morally the Gentleman by Creation may be the better; for the other may be a Debauch'd man, this a Person of worth.

2. Gentlemen have ever been more Temperate in their Religion, than the Common People, as having more Reason, the others running in a hurry. In the beginning of Christianity, the Fathers writ *Contra gentes*, and *Contra Gentiles*, they were all one: But after all were Christians, the better sort of People still retain'd the name of Gentiles, throughout the four Provinces of the *Roman Empire;* as *Gentilhomme* in *French*, *Gentilhomo* in *Italian*, *Gentilhuombre* in *Spanish*, and *Gentil-man* in *English*: And they, no question, being Persons of Quality, kept up those Feasts which we borrow from the Gentils; as *Christmas*, *Candlemas*, *May day*, &c. continuing what was not directly against Christianity, which the Common people would never have endured.

Gold.

1. THere are two Reasons, why these words *(Jesus autem transiens per medium eorum ibat)* were about our old Gold: the one is, because *Ripley* the Alchymist, when he made Gold in the *Tower*, the first time he found it, he spoke these words [*per medium eorum*] that is, *per medium ignis, et Sulphuris*. The other, because these words were thought to be a Charm, and that they did bind whatsoever they were written upon, so that a Man could not take it away. To this Reason I rather incline.

Hall.

1. THE Hall was the place where the great Lord us'd to eat, (wherefore elfe were the Halls made fo big?) Where he faw all his Servants and Tenants about him. He eat not in private, Except in time of ficknefs; when once he became a thing Coopt up, all his greatnefs was fpoil'd. Nay the King himfelf ufed to eat in the Hall, and his Lords fate with him, and then he underflood Men.

Hell.

1. THere are two Texts for Chrift's defcending into Hell: The one *Pfalm*. 16. The other *Acts* the 2*d*. where the Bible that was in ufe when the thirty nine Articles were made has it (*Hell*.) But the Bible that was in Queen *Elisabeth*'s time, when the Articles were confirm'd, reads it (*Grave*,) and fo it continu'd till the New Tranflation in King *James*'s time, and then 'tis *Hell* again. But by this we may gather the Church of *England* declined as much as they could, the defcent, otherwife they never would have alter'd the Bible.

2. (*He defcended into Hell*) this may be the Interpretation of it. He may be dead and buried, then his Soul afcended into Heaven. Afterwards he defcended again into *Hell*, that is, into the Grave, to fetch his Body, and to rife again. The ground of this Interpretation is taken from the Platonick Learning, who held a Metempfychofis, and when a Soul did defcend from Heaven to take another Body, they call'd it κατά βάσιν εἰς ᾅδην taking ᾅδης. for the lower World, the ftate of Mortality: Now the firft Chriftians many of them were Platonick Philofophers, and no queftion fpake fuch Language as then was underftood amongft them. To underftand by *Hell* the Grave is no Tautology, becaufe the Creed firft tells what Chrift fuffer'd, *he was Crucified, Dead, and Buried*; then it tells us what he did, *he defcended into Hell, the third day he rofe again, he afcended, &c.*

Holy-days.

1. They say the Church imposes Holy-days, there's no such thing, though the number of Holy-days is set down in some of our Common-Prayer Books. Yet that has relation to an Act of Parliament, which forbids the keeping of any Holy-Days in time of Popery, but those that are kept, are kept by the Custom of the Country, and I hope you will not say the Church imposes that.

Humility.

1. Humility is a Vertue all preach, none practise, and yet every body is content to hear. The Master thinks it good Doctrine for his Servant, the Laity for the Clergy, and the Clergy for the Laity.

2. There is *Humilitas quædam in Vitio*. If a man does not take notice of that excellency and perfection that is in himself, how can he be thankful to God, who is the Author of all Excellency and Perfection? Nay, if a Man hath too mean an Opinion of himself, 'twill render him unserviceable both to God and Man.

3. Pride may be allow'd to this or that degree, else a man cannot keep up his Dignity. In Gluttons there must be Eating, in drunkenness there must be drinking; 'tis not the eating, nor 'tis not the drinking that is to be blam'd, but the Excess. So in Pride.

Idolatry.

1. Idolatry is in a Man's own thought, not in the Opinion of another. Put Case I bow to the Altar, why am I guilty of Idolatry? because a stander by thinks so? I am sure I do not believe the Altar to be God, and the God I worship may be bow'd to in all places, and at all times.

Jews.

1. God at the first gave Laws to all Mankind, but afterwards he gave peculiar Laws to the Jews, which they were only to observe. Just

as we have the Common Law for all *England*, and yet you have some Corporations, that, besides that, have peculiar Laws and priviledges to themselves.

2. Talk what you will of the Jews, that they are Cursed, they thrive where e're they come, they are able to oblige the Prince of their Country by lending him money, none of them beg, they keep together, and for their being hated, my life for yours, Christians hate one another as much.

Invincible Ignorance.

'TIS all one to me if I am told of Christ, or some Mystery of Christianity, if I am not capable of understanding, as if I am not told at all, my Ignorance is as invincible, and therefore 'tis vain to call their Ignorance only invincible, who never were told of Christ. The trick of it is to advance the Priest, whilst the Church of *Rome* says a Man must be told of Christ, by one thus and thus ordain'd.

Images.

1. THE Papists taking away the second [Commandment], is not haply so horrid a thing, nor so unreasonable amongst Christians as we make it. For the *Jews* could make no figure of God, but they must commit Idolatry, because he had taken no shape, but since the Assumption of our flesh we know what shape to picture God in. Nor do I know why we may not make his Image, provided we be sure what it is: as we say Saint *Luke* took the picture of the Virgin *Mary*, and Saint *Veronica* of our Saviour. Otherwise it would be no honour to the King, to make a Picture, and call it the King's Picture, when 'tis nothing like him.

2. Though the Learned Papists pray not to Images, yet 'tis to be feared the ignorant do; as appears by that Story of St. *Nicholas* in *Spain*. A Countrey-man us'd to offer daily to St. *Nicholas*'s Image, at length by mischance the Image was broken, and a new one made of his own Plumb-Tree; after that the man forbore, being complain'd of to his Ordinary, he answer'd, 'tis

true, he us'd to offer to the Old Image, but to the new he could not find in his heart, becaufe he knew 'twas a piece of his own Plumb Tree. You fee what Opinion this man had of the Image, and to this tended the bowing of their Images, the twinkling of their Eyes, the Virgins Milk, &c. Had they only meant reprefentations, a Picture would have done as well as thefe tricks. It may be with us in *England* they do not worfhip images, becaufe living among
they are either laught out of it, or beaten out of i fhock of Argument.

3. 'Tis a difcreet way concerning Pictures in Churches, to fet up no new, nor to pull down no old.

Imperial Constitutions.

1. THey fay Imperial Conftitutions did only confirm the Canons of the Church, but that is not fo, for they inflicted punifhment, when the Canons never did. (*viz.*) If a man Converted a Chriftian to be a Jew, he was to forfeit his Eftate, and lofe his Life. In *Valentines* Novels 'tis faid. *Epifcopus Forum Legibus non habere, et Judicant tantum de Religione.*

Imprisonment.

1. SIR *Kenelme Digby* was feveral times taken and let go again, at laft Imprifon'd in *Winchefter-Houfe*. I can compare him to nothing a great Fifh that we catch and let go again, but ftill he will come to the Bait, at laft therefore we put him into fome great Pond for Store.

Incendiaries.

1. FAncy to your felf a Man fets the City on Fire at *Cripplegate*, and that Fire continues by means of others, 'till it come to *White-Fryers*, and then he that began it would fain quench it, does not he deferve to be punifht moft that firft fet the City on Fire? So 'tis with the Incendiaries of the State. They that firft fet it on fire [by Monopolizing, Forreft *Bufinefs*, Imprifoning Parliament Men, *tertio Caroli,*

&c.] are now become regenerate, and would fain quench the Fire; Certainly they deferv'd moſt to be puniſh'd, for being the firſt Cauſe of our Diſtractions.

Independency.

1. INdependency is in uſe at *Amſterdam*, where forty Churches or Congregations have nothing to do one with another. And 'tis no queſtion agreeable to the Primitive times, before the Emperour became Chriſtian. For either we muſt ſay every Church govern'd it ſelf, or elſe we muſt fall upon that old fooliſh Rock, that St. *Peter* and his Succeſſours govern'd all, but when the Civil State became Chriſtian, they appointed who ſhould govern them, before they govern'd by agreement and conſent; if you will not do this, you ſhall come no more amongſt us, but both the Independant man, and the Presbyterian man do equally exclude the Civil Power, though after a different manner.

2. The Independant may as well plead, they ſhould not be ſubject to temporal Things, not come before a Conſtable, or a Juſtice of Peace, as they plead they ſhould not be ſubject in Spiritual things, becauſe St *Paul* ſays, *Is it ſo, that there is not a wiſe man amongſt you?*

3. The Pope challenges all Churches to be under him, the King and the two Arch-Biſhops challenge all the Church of *England* to be under them. The Presbyterian man divides the Kingdom into as many Churches as there be Presbyteries, and your Independant would have every Congregation a Church by it ſelf.

Things Indifferent.

1. IN a time of Parliament, when things are under debate, they are indifferent, but in a Church or State ſetled, there's nothing left indifferent.

Publick Intereſt.

1. ALL might go well in the Common-Wealth, if every one in the Parliament would lay down his own Intereſt, and aim at the general good. If a man were ſick, and the whole Colledge of

Phyſicians ſhould come to him, and adminiſter ſeverally, haply ſo long as they obſerv'd the Rules of Art he might recover, but if one of them had a great deal of Scamony by him, he muſt put off that, therefore he preſcribes Scamony. Another had a great deal of Rubarb, and he muſt put off that, and therefore he preſcribes Rubarb, &c. they would certainly kill the man. We deſtroy the Common-wealth, while we pre- ſerve our own private Intereſts, and neglect the Publick.

Humane Invention.

1. YOU ſay there muſt be no Human Invention in the Church, nothing but the pure word. *Anſwer.* If I give any Expoſition, but what is expreſs'd in the Text, that is my invention: if you give another Expoſition, that is your invention, and both are Human. For Example, ſuppoſe the word [Egg] were in the Text, I ſay, 'tis meant an Henn-Egg, you ſay a Gooſe-Egg, neither of theſe are expreſt, therefore they are Humane Invention, and I am ſure the newer the Invention the worſe, old Inventions are heſt.

2. If we muſt admit nothing, but what we read in the Bible, what will become of the Parliament? for we do not read of that there.

Judgments.

1. WE cannot tell what is a Judgment of God, 'tis preſumption to take upon us to know. In time of Plague we know we want health, and therefore we pray to God to give us health, in time of War we know we want peace, and therefore we pray to God to give us peace. Commonly we ſay a Judgment falls upon a man for ſomething in them we cannot abide. An Example we have in King *James*, concerning the death of *Henry* the Fourth of *France*; one ſaid he was kill'd for his Wenching, an- other ſaid he was kill'd for turning his Religion. No, ſays King *James* (who could not abide fighting) he was kill'd for permitting Duels in his Kingdom.

Judge.

1. WE see the Pageants in *Cheapside*, the Lions, and the Elephants, but we do not see the men that carry them; we see the Judges look big, look like Lions, but we do not see who moves them.

2. Little things do great works, when great things will not. If I should take a Pin from the ground, a little pair of Tongues will do it, when a great pair will not. Go to a Judge to do a business for you, by no means he will not hear it; but go to some small Servant about him, and he dispatch it according to your hearts desire.

3. There could be no mischief done in the Commonwealth without a Judge. Though there be false Dice brought in at the Groom-Porters, and cheating offer'd, yet unless he allow the Cheating, and judge the Dice to be good, there may be hopes of fair play.

Juggling.

1. 'TIS not Juggling that is to be blam'd, but much Juggling, for the World cannot be Govern'd without it. All your Rhetorick, and all your Elenchs in Logick come within the compass of Juggling.

Jurisdiction.

1. THere's no such Thing as Spiritual Jurisdiction, all is Civil, the Churches is the same with the Lord Mayors; suppose a Christian came into a Pagan Country, how can you fancy he shall have any Power there? he finds faults with the Gods of the Country, well, they will put him to Death for it, when he is a Martyr, what follows? Does that argue he has any Spiritual Jurisdiction? If the Clergy say the Church ought to be govern'd thus, and thus, by the word of God, that is Doctrine all, that is not Discipline.

2. The Pope he challenges Jurisdiction over all, the Bishops they pretend to it as well as he, the Presbyterians they would have it to themselves, but over whom is all this? the poor Laymen.

Jus Divinum.

1. ALL things are held by *Jus Divinum*, either immediately or mediately.

2. Nothing has lost the Pope so much in his Supremacy, as not acknowledging what Princes gave him. 'Tis a scorn upon the Civil Power, and an unthankfulness in the Priest. But the Church runs to *Jus Divinum*, lest if they should acknowledge what they have they have by positive Law, it might be as well taken from them as given to them.

King.

1. A King is a thing men have made for their own sakes, for quietness sake. Just as in a Family one Man is appointed to buy Meat; if every one should buy, or if there were many buyers, they would never agree, one would buy what the other lik'd not, or what the other had bought before, so there would be a confusion. But that Charge being committed to one, he according to his Discretion pleases all, if they have not what they would have one day, they shall have it the next, or something as good.

2. The word King directs our Eyes, suppose it had been Consul, or Dictator, to think all Kings alike is the same folly, as if a Consul of *Aleppo* or *Smyrna*, should claim to himself the same power that a Consul at *Rome*, What, am not I a Consul? or a Duke of *England* should think himself like the Duke of *Florence*; nor can it be imagin'd, that the word βασιλὺς did signifie the same in Greek, as the Hebrew word כלך did with the *Jews*. Besides, let the Divines in their Pulpits say what they will, they in their practice deny that all is the Kings: They sue him, and so does all the Nation, whereof they are a part. What matter is it then, what they Preach or what they Teach in the Schools?

3. Kings are all individual, this or that King, there is no Species of Kings.

4. A King that claims Priviledges in his own Country, because they have them in another, is just as a Cook, that

liv'd there, and he had alſo the Abbot and his Monks, and all theſe the King's Houſe.

5. The Three Eſtates are the Lords Temporal, the Biſhops are the Clergy, and the Commons, as ſome would have it [take heed of that] for then if two agree the third is involv'd, but he is King of the Three Eſtates.

6. The King hath a Seal in every Court, and the Great Seal be call'd *Sigillum Angliæ*, the Great of *England*, yet 'tis not becauſe 'tis the Kingdoms and not the Kings, but to diſtinguiſh it from *Sigillum Hiberniæ, Sigillum Scotiæ*.

7. The Court of *England* is much alter'd. At a ſolemn Dancing, firſt you had the grave Meaſures, then the Corrantoes and the Galliards, and this is kept up with Ceremony, at length to *French*-more, and the Cuſhion-Dance, and then all the Company Dance, Lord and Groom, Lady and Kitchin-Maid, no diſtinction. So in our Court in Queen *Elizabeth*'s time Gravity and State were kept up. In King *James*'s time things were pretty well. But in King *Charles*'s time, there has been nothing but *French*-more and the Cuſhion Dance, *omnium gatherum*, tolly, polly, hoite come toite.

The King.

1. 'TIS hard to make an accommodation between the King and the Parliament. If you and I fell out out about Money, you ſaid I ow'd you twenty Pounds, I ſaid I ow'd you but ten Pounds, it may be a third Party allowing me Twenty Marks, might make us Friends. But if I ſaid I ow'd you twenty Pounds in Silver, and you ſaid I ow'd you twenty pound of Diamonds, which is a ſum innumerable, 'tis impoſſible we ſhould ever agree, this is the caſe.

2. The King uſing the Houſe of Commons, as he did in Mr. *Pymm* and his Company, that is charging Treaſon, becauſe they charg'd my Lord of *Canterbury* and Sir *George Ratcliff*, it was juſt with as much Logick as the Boy, that would have lain with his

Grandmother, us'd to his Father, you lay with my Mother, why ſhould not I lye with yours?

3. There is not the ſame reaſon for the King's accuſing Men of Treaſon, and carrying them away, as there is for the Houſes themſelves, becauſe they accuſe one of themſelves. For every one that is accuſed, is either a Peer or a Commoner, and he that is accuſed hath his Conſent going along with him; but if the King accuſes, there is nothing of this in it.

4. The King is equally abus'd now as before, then they flatter'd him and made him do ill things, now they would force him againſt his Conſcience. If a Phiſician ſhould tell me, every thing I had a mind to was good for me, tho' in truth 'twas Poiſon, he abus'd me; and he abuſes me as much, that would force me to take ſomething whether I will or no.

5. The King ſo long as he is our King, may do with his Officers what he pleaſes, as the Maſter of the Houſe may turn away all his Servants, and take whom he pleaſe.

6. The King's Oath is not ſecurity enough for our Property, for he ſwears to Govern according to Law; now the Judges they interpret the Law, and what Judges can be made to do we know.

7. The King and the Parliament now falling out, are juſt as when there is foul Play offer'd amongſt Gameſters, one ſnatches the others ſtake, they ſeize what they can of one anothers. 'Tis not to be askt whether it belongs not to the King to do this or that; before when there was fair Play, it did. But now they will do what is moſt convenient for their own ſafety. If two fall to ſcuffling, one tears the others Band, the other tears his, when they were Friends they were quiet, and did no ſuch thing, they let one anothers Bands alone.

8. The King calling his Friends from the Parliament, becauſe he had uſe of them at *Oxford*, is as if a man ſhould have uſe of a little piece of wood, and he runs down into the Cellar, and takes the Spiggott, in the mean time all the Beer runs about the Houſe, when his Friends are abſent the King will be loſt.

Knights-Service.

1. KNights-Service in earnest means nothing, for the Lords are bound to wait upon the King when he goes to War with a Foreign Enemy, with it may be One Man and One Horse, and he that doth not, is to be rated so much as shall seem good to the next Parliament. And what will that be? So 'tis for a private Man, that holds of a Gentleman.

Land.

1. WHen men did let their Land underfoot, the Tenants would fight for their Landlords, so that way they had their Retribution, but now they will do nothing for them, may be the first, if but a Constable bid them, that shall lay the Landlord by the heels, and therefore 'tis vanity and folly not to take the full value.

2. *Allodium* is a Law-word contrary to *Feudum*, and it signifies Land that holds of no body, we have no such Land in *England*. 'Tis a true Proposition, all the Land in *England* is held, either immediately, or mediately of the King.

Language.

1. TO a living Tongue new words may be added, but not to a dead Tongue, as Latine, Greek, Hebrew, &c.

2. *Latimer* is the Corruption of *Latiner*, it signifies he that interprets Latine, and though he interpreted *French, Spanish*, or *Italian*, he was call'd the King's *Latiner*, that is, the King's Interpreter.

3. If you look upon the Language spoken in the Saxon time, and the Language spoken now, you will find the difference to be just, as if a man had a Cloak that he wore plain in Queen *Elisabeth's* days, and since, here has put in a piece of Red, and there a piece of Blew, and here a piece of Green, and there a piece of Orange-tawny. We borow words from the *French, Italian, Latine*, as every Pedantick man pleases.

4. We have more words than Notions, half a dozen words for the fame thing. Sometime we put a new fignification to an old word, as when we call a Piece a Gun. The word Gun was in ufe in *England* for an Engine to caft a thing from a man, long before there was any Gun-powder found out.

5. Words muft be fitted to a man's mouth; 'twas well faid of the Fellow that was to make a Speech for my Lord Mayor, he defir'd to take meafure of his Lordfhips mouth.

Law.

1. A Man may plead not guilty, and yet tell no Lye, for by the Law no Man is bound to accufe himfelf, fo that when I fay Not guilty, the meaning is, as if I fhould fay by way of Paraphrafe, I am Not fo guilty as to tell you; if you will bring me to a Tryal, and have me punifht for this you lay to my Charge, prove it againft me.

2. Ignorance of the Law excufes no man, not that all Men know the Law, but becaufe 'tis an excufe every man will plead, and no man can tell how to confute him.

3. The King of *Spain* was out-law'd in *Weftminfter-Hall*, I being of Council againft him. A Merchant had recover'd Cofts againft him in a Suit, which becaufe he could not get, we advis'd to have him Out-law'd for not appearing, and fo he was. As foon as *Gondimer* heard that, he prefently fent the money, by reafon, if his Mafter had been Out-law'd he could not have the benefit of the Law, which would have been very prejudicial, there being then many fuits depending betwixt the King of *Spain* and our Englifh Merchants.

4. Every Law is a Contract between the King and the People, and therefore to be kept. An hundred men may owe me an hundred pounds, as well as any one man, and fhall they not pay me becaufe they are ftronger than I? *Object.* Oh but they lofe all if they keep that Law. *Anfw.* Let them look to the making of their Bargain. If I fell my Lands, and when I have done, one comes and tells me I have nothing elfe to keep me. I and my Wife and Children muft ftarve,

if I part with my Land. Muft I not therefore let them have my Land that have bought it and paid for it?

5. The Parliament may declare Law, as well as any other inferior Court may, (*viz.*) the Kings Bench. In that or this particular Cafe the Kings Bench will declare unto you what the Law is, but that binds no body whom the Cafe concerns: So the higheft Court, the Parliament may doe, but not declare Law, that is, make Law that was never heard of before.

Law of Nature.

1. I Cannot fancy to my felf what the Law of Nature means, but the Law of God. How fhould I know I ought not to fteal, I ought not to commit Adultery, unlefs fome body had told me fo? Surely 'tis becaufe I have been told fo? 'Tis not becaufe I think I ought not to do them, nor becaufe you think I ought not; if fo, our minds might change, whence then comes the reftraint? from a higher Power, nothing elfe can bind. I cannot bind myfelf, for I may untye my felf again; nor an equal cannot bind me, for we may untie one another. It muft be a fuperiour Power, even God Almighty. If two of us make a Bargain, why fhould either of us ftand to it? What need you care what you fay, or what need I care what I fay? Certainly becaufe there is fomething about me that tells me *Fides eft fervanda*, and if we after alter our minds, and make a new Bargain, there's *Fides fervanda* there too.

Learning.

1. NO man is the wifer for his Learning, it may Adminifter matter to work in, or Objects to work upon, but Wit and Wifdom are born with a Man.

2. Moft mens Learning is nothing but Hiftory duly taken up. If I quote *Thomas Aquinus* for fome Tenet and believe it, becaufe the Schoolmen fay fo, that is but Hiftory. Few men make themfelves Mafters of the things they write or fpeak.

3. The Jesuits and the Lawyers of *France*, and the Low-Country-men have engrossed all Learning. The rest of the world make nothing but Homilies.

4. 'Tis observable, that in *Athens* where the Arts flourisht, they were govern'd by a Democrasie, Learning made them think themselves as wise as any body, and they would govern as well as others; and they spake as it were by way of Contempt, that in the *East* and in the *North* they had Kings, and why? Because the most part of them follow'd their business, and if some one man had made himself wiser than the rest, he govern'd them, and they willingly submitted themselves to him. *Aristotle* makes the Observation. And as in *Athens* the Philosophers made the People knowing, and therefore they thought themselves wise enough to govern, so does preaching with us, and that makes us affect a Democrasie: For upon these two grounds we all would be Governours, either because we think our selves as wise as the best, or because we think our selves the Elect, and have the Spirit, and the rest a Company of Reprobates that belong to the Devil.

Lecturers.

1. LEcturers do in a Parish Church what the Fryers did heretofore, get away not only the Affections, but the Bounty, that should be bestow'd upon the Minister.

2. Lecturers get a great deal of money, because they preach the People tame [as a man watches a Hawk] and then they do what they list with them.

3. The Lectures in Black Fryers, perform'd by Officers of the Army, Trades-men, and Ministers, is as if a great Lord should make a Feast, and he would have his Cook dress one Dish, and his Coachman another, his Porter a third, &c.

Libels.

1. THO' some make slight of *Libels*, yet you may see by them how the wind sits: As take a straw and throw it up into the Air, you shall see by that which way the Wind is, which you

Liturgy.

1. There is no Church without a Liturgy, nor indeed can there be conveniently, as there is no School without a Grammar. One Scholar may be taught otherwife upon the Stock of his Acumen, but not a whole School. One or two that are pioufly difpos'd, may ferve themfelves their own way, but hardly a whole Nation.

2. To know what was generally believ'd in all Ages, the way is to confult the Liturgies, not any private man's writing. As if you would know how the Church of *England* ferves God. Go to the Common prayer-Book, confult not this nor that man. Befides Liturgies never Complement, nor ufe high Expreffions. The Fathers oft-times fpeak Oratorioufly.

Lords in the Parliament.

1. The Lords giving Protections is a fcorn upon them. A Protection means nothing actively, but paffively, he that is a Servant to a Parliament man is thereby Protected. What a fcorn is it to a perfon of Honour to put his hand to two Lyes at once, that fuch a man is my Servant, and imployed by me, when haply he never faw the man in his life, nor before never heard of him.

2. The Lords protefting is foolifh. To proteft is properly to fave to a man's felf fome right. But to proteft as the Lords proteft, when they their felves are involv'd, 'tis no more than if I fhould go into *Smithfield,* and fell my Horfe, and take the money, and yet when I have your Money, and you my Horfe, I fhould proteft this Horfe is mine, becaufe I love the Horfe, or I do not know why I do proteft, becaufe my Opinion is contrary to the reft. Ridiculous, when they fay the Bifhops did antiently proteft, it was only *diffenting,* and that in the cafe of the Pope.

Lords before the Parliament.

1. GReat Lords by reafon of their Flatterers, are the firſt that know their own Vertues, and the laſt that know their own Vices; Some of them are aſham'd upwards, becauſe their Anceſtors were too great. Others are aſham'd downwards, becauſe they were too little.

2. The *Priour* of St *John* of *Jeruſalem* is ſaid to be *Primus Baro Angliæ*, the firſt Baron of *England*, becauſe being laſt of the Spiritual Barons, he choſe to be firſt of the Temporal. He was a kind of an Otter, a Knight half-Spiritual, and half-Temporal.

3. *Queſt.* Whether is every Baron a Baron of ſome place?
Anſw. 'Tis according to his Patent, of late years they have been made Baron of ſome place, but antiently not, call'd only by their Sir-name, or the Sir-name of ſome Family, into which they have been married.

4. The making of new Lords leſſens all the reſt. 'Tis in the buſineſs of Lords, as 'twas with St. *Nicholas*'s Image; the Countryman, you know, could not find in his heart to adore the new Image, made of his own Plumb-Tree, though he had formerly Worſhip'd the old one. The Lords that are antient we honour, becauſe we know not whence they come, but the new ones we ſlight, becauſe we know their beginning.

5. For the *Iriſh* Lords to take upon them here in *England;* is as if the Cook in the Fair ſhould come to my Lady *Kents* kitchen, and take upon him to roaſt the meat there, becauſe he is a Cook in another place.

Marriage.

1. OF all Actions of a man's life, his Marriage does leaſt concern other people, yet of all Actions of our Life, 'tis moſt medled with by other people.

2. Marriage is nothing but a Civil Contract, 'tis true 'tis an Ordinance of God: ſo is every other Contract, God commands me to keep it when I have made it.

3. Marriage is a deſperate thing, the Frogs in *Æſop* were extream wiſe, they had a great mind to ſome

a Medlar that is rotten, and 'tis a fine thing, and yet I'le warrant you the Pear thinks as well of it self as the Medlar does.

2. We measure the Excellency of other men, by some Excellency we conceive to be in our selves. *Nash* a Poet, poor enough (as Poets us'd to be) seeing an Alderman with his Gold Chain, upon his great Horse, by way of scorn said to one of his Companions, do you see yon fellow, how goodly, how big he looks, why that fellow cannot make a blank Verse.

3. Nay we measure the goodness of God from ourselves, we measure his Goodness, his Justice, his Wisdom, by something we call just, good, or wise in our selves; and in so doing we judge proportionably to the Country fellow in the Play, who said if he were a King, he would live like a Lord, and have Pease and Bacon every day, and a Whip that cry'd Slash.

Difference of Men.

1. THE difference of men is very great, you would scarce think them to be of the same Species, and yet it consists more in the Affection than in the Intellect. For as in the strength of Body, two men shall be of an equal strength, yet one shall appear stronger than the other, because he exercises, and puts out his strength, the other will not stir nor strain himself. So 'tis in the strength of the Brain, the one endeavours, and strains, and labours, and studies, the other sits still, and is idle, and takes no pains, and therefore he appears so much the inferiour.

Minister Divine.

1. THE imposition of hands upon the Minister when all is done, will be nothing but a designation of a Person to this or that Office or Employment in the Church. 'Tis a ridiculous Phrase that of the Canonists [*Conferre Ordines*] 'Tis *Coaptare aliquem in Ordinem*, to make a man one of us, one of our Number, one of our Order. So *Cicero* would understand what I said, it being a Phrase borrow'd from the *Latines*, and

to be underſtood proportionably to what was amongſt them.

2. Thoſe words you now uſe in making a Miniſter [*receive the Holy Ghoſt*] were us'd amongſt the *Jews* in making of a Lawyer, from thence we have them, which is a villanous key to ſomething, as if you would have ſome other kind of Præfeture, than a Mayoralty, and yet keep the ſame Ceremony that was us'd in making the Mayor.

3. A Prieſt has no ſuch thing as an indelible Character, what difference do you find betwixt him and another man after Ordination? only he is made a Prieſt, (as I ſaid) by Deſignation: as a Lawyer is call'd to the Bar, then made a Serjeant; all men that would get power over others, make themſelves as unlike them as they can, upon the ſame ground the Prieſts made themſelves unlike the Laity.

4. A Miniſter when he is made is *Materia prima*, apt for any form the State will put upon him, but of himſelf he can do nothing. Like a Doctor of Law in the Univerſity, he hath a great deal of Law in him, but cannot uſe it till he be made ſome bodies Chancellour; or like a Phyſician, before he be receiv'd into a houſe, he can give no body Phyſick; indeed after the Maſter of the houſe hath given him charge of his Servants, then he may. Or like a Suffragan, that could do nothing but give Orders, and yet was no Biſhop.

5. A Miniſter ſhould preach according to the Articles of Religion Eſtabliſhed in the Church where he is. To be a Civil Lawyer let a man read *Juſtinian*, and the Body of the Law, to confirm his Brain to that way, but when he comes to practice, he muſt make uſe of it ſo far as it concerns the Law received in his own Country. To be a Phyſician let a Man read *Gallen* and *Hypocrates;* but when he practices, he muſt apply his Medicines according to the Temper of thoſe Mens Bodies with whom he lives, and have reſpect to the heat and cold of Climes, otherwiſe that which in *Pergamus* (where *Gallen* liv'd) was Phyſick, in our cold *Climate* may be Poiſon. So to be a Divine, let him

read the whole Body of Divinity, the Fathers and the Schoolmen, but when he comes to practice, he must use it and apply it according to thofe Grounds and Articles of Religion that are eftablifh'd in the Church, and this with fence.

6. There be four things a Minifter fhould be at, the Confcionary part, Ecclefiaftical ftory, School Divinity, and the Cafuifts.

1. In the Confcionary part he muft read all the Chief Fathers, both Latine and Greek wholly. St. *Auftin*, St. *Ambrofe*, St. *Chryfoftome*, both the *Gregories, &c. Tertullian, Clemens, Alexandrinus*, and *Epiphanius*, which laft have more Learning in them than all the reft, and writ freely.

2. For Ecclefiaftical ftory let him read *Baronius*, with the *Magdeburgenfes*, and be his own Judge, the one being extreamly for the Papifts, the other extreamly againft them.

3. For School Divinity let him get *Javellus*'s Edition of *Scotus* or *Mayro*, where there be Quotations that direct you to every Schoolman, where fuch and fuch queftions are handled. Without School-Divinity a Divine knows nothing Logically, nor will be able to fatisfie a rational man out of the Pulpit.

4. The Study of the Cafuifts muft follow the Study of the School-men, becaufe the divifion of their Cafes is according to their Divinity, otherwife he that begins with them will know little. As he that begins with the ftudy of the Reports and Cafes in the Common Law, will thereby know little of the Law. Cafuifts may be of admirable ufe, if difcreetly dealt with, tho' among them you fhall have many leaves together very impertinent. A Cafe well decided would ftick by a man, they would remember it whether they will or no, whereas a quaint pofition dieth in the Birth. The main thing is to know where to fearch, for talk what they will of vaft memories, no man will prefume upon his own memory for any thing he means to write or fpeak in publick.

7. [*Go and teach all Nations.*] This was faid to all

may lye and ftarve, and rot, before any body will look after you.

12. Methinks 'tis an ignorant thing for a Churchman, to call himfelf the Minifter of Chrift, becaufe St. *Paul*, or the Apoftles call'd themfelves fo. If one of them had a Voice from Heav'n, as St. *Paul* had, I will grant he is a Minifter of Chrift, I will call him fo too. Muft they take upon them as the Apoftles did? Can they do as the Apoftles could? The Apoftles had a Mark to be known by, fpake Tongues, Cur'd Difeafes, trod upon Serpents, &c. Can they do this? If a Gentleman tells me, he will fend his Man to me, and I did not know his Man, but he gave me this Mark to know him by, he fhould bring in his hand a rich Jewel; if a fellow came to me with a pebble-Stone, had I any reafon to believe he was the Gentleman's man?

Money.

1. MOney makes a man laugh. A blind Fidler playing to a Company, and playing but fcurvily, the Company laught at him; His Boy that led him, perceiving it, cry'd, Father let us be gone, they do nothing but laugh at you. Hold thy peace, Boy, faid the Fidler, we fhall have their money prefently, and then we will laugh at them.

2. *Euclide* was beaten in *Boccaline*, for teaching his Scholars a Mathematical Figure in his School, whereby he fhew'd, that all the Lives both of Princes and private Men tended to one Centre, *Con Gentilizza*, handfomly to get money out of other mens pockets, and it into their own.

3. The Pope us'd heretofore to fend the Princes of Chriftendom to fight againft the *Turk*, but Prince and Pope finely Juggl'd together, the Moneys were rais'd, and fome men went out to the Holy War, but commonly after they had got the money, the Turk was pretty quiet, and the Prince and the Pope fhar'd it between them.

4. In all times the Princes in *England* have done fomething illegal, to get money. But then came

a Parliament and all was well, the People and the Prince kiſt and were Friends, and ſo things were quiet for a while; afterwards there was another trick found out to get money, and after they had got it, another Parliament was call'd to ſet all right, &c. But now they have ſo out-run the Conſtable————

Moral Honesty.

1. THey that cry down Moral-honeſty, cry down that which is a great part of Religion, my Duty towards God, and my Duty towards man. What care I to ſee a man run after a Sermon, if he Couzen and Cheats as ſoon as he comes home. On the other ſide Morality muſt not be without Religion, for if ſo, it may change, as I ſee convenience. Religion muſt govern it. He that has not Religion to govern his Morality, is not a Dram better than my Maſtiff-Dogg; ſo long as you ſtroak him and pleaſe him, and do not pinch him, he will play with you as finely as may be, he is a very good Moral-Maſtiff, but if you hurt him, he will fly in your Face, and tear out your Throat.

Mortgage.

1. IN Caſe I receive a thouſand pounds, and Mortgage as much Land as is worth two thouſand to you, if I do not pay the Money at ſuch a day, I fail, whether you may take my Land and keep it in point of Conſcience? *Anſw.* If you had my Lands as ſecurity only for your Money, then you are not to keep it, but if we bargain'd ſo, that if I did not repay your 1000*l.* my Land ſhould go for it, be it what it will, no doubt you may with a ſafe Conſcience keep it; for in theſe things all the Obligation is *Servare Fidem.*

Number.

1. ALL thoſe miſterious things they obſerve in numbers, come to nothing, upon this very ground, becauſe number in it ſelf is nothing, has not *to do with* Nature, but is merely of Human Impoſition,

a meer found. For Example, when I cry one a Clock, two a Clock, three a Clock, that is but Man's divifion of time, the time it felf goes on, and it had been all one in Nature if thofe Hours had been call'd nine, ten, and eleven. So when they fay the Seventh Son is Fortunate, it means nothing; for if you count from the feventh back-wards, then the firft is the seventh, why is not he likewife Fortunate?

Oaths.

1. SWearing was another thing with the *Jews* than with us, becaufe they might not pronounce the Name of the Lord Jehovah.

2. There is no Oath fcarcely, but we fwear to things we are ignorant of: For Example, the Oath of Supremacy: how many know how the King is King? what are his Right and Prerogative? So how many know what are the Priviledges of the Parliament, and the Liberty of the Subject, when they take the proteftation? But the meaning is, they will defend them when they know them. As if I fhould fwear I would take part with all that wear Red Ribbons in their Hats, it may be I do not know which colour is Red; but when I do know, and fee a Red Ribbon in a Man's Hat, then will I take his part.

3. I cannot conceive how an Oath is impofed, where there is a Parity (*vis.*) in the Houfe of Commons, they are all *pares inter fe*, only one brings Paper, and fhews it the reft, they look upon it, and in their own Sence take it: Now they are but *pares* to me, who am none of the Houfe, for I do not acknowledge my felf their Subject, if I did, then no queftion, I was bound by an Oath of their impofing. 'Tis to me but reading a Paper in their own Sence.

4. There is a great difference between an Affertory Oath and a Promiffary Oath. An Affertory Oath is made to a Man before God, and I Muft fwear fo, as man may know what I mean: But a Promiffary Oath is made to God only, and I am fure he knows my meaning; So in the new Oath it runs [whereas I be-

Oracles.

1. ORacles ceas'd prefently after Chrift, as foon as nobody believ'd them. Juft as we have no Fortune-Tellers, nor Wife-Men, when no body cares for them. Sometime you have a Seafon for them, when People believe them, and neither of thefe, I conceive, wrought by the Devil.

Opinion.

1. OPinion and Affection extremely differ; I may affect a Woman beft, but it does not follow I muft think her the Handfomeft Woman in the World. I love Apples the beft of any Fruit, but it does not follow, I muft think Apples to be the beft Fruit. Opinion is fomething wherein I go about to give Reafon why all the World fhould think as I think. Affection is a thing wherein I look after the pleafing of my felf.

2. 'Twas a good Fancy of an old Platonick: The Gods which are above men, had fomething whereof Man did partake, [an Intellect Knowledge] and the Gods kept on their courfe quietly. The Beafts, which are below man, had fomething whereof Man did partake, [Sence and Growth,] and the Beafts liv'd quietly in their way. But Man had fomething in him, whereof neither Gods nor Beafts did partake, which gave him all the Trouble, and made all the Confufion in the world, and that is Opinion.

3. 'Tis a foolifh thing for me to be brought off from an Opinion in a thing neither of us know, but are led only by fome Cobweb-stuff, as in fuch a cafe as this, *Utrum Angeli in vicem colloquantur?* if I forfake my fide in fuch a cafe, I fhew my felf wonderful light, or infinitely complying, or flattering the other party. But if I be in a bufinefs of Nature, and hold an Opinion one way, and fome man's Experience has found out the contrary, I may with a fafe Reputation give up my fide.

4. 'Tis a vain thing to talk of an Heretick, for a man for his heart can think no otherwife than he does think. In the Primitive times there were many Opinions, nothing fcarce but fome or other held: One of thefe Opinions being embrac'd by fome Prince, and received into his Kingdom, the reft were Condemn'd as Herefies, and his Religion which was but one of the feveral Opinions, firft is faid to be Orthodox, and fo have continu'd ever fince the Apoftles.

Parity.

1. This is the juggling trick of the Parity, they would have no body above them, but they do not tell you they would have no body under them.

Parliament.

1. All are involved in a Parliament. There was a time when all Men had their voice in choofing Knights. About *Henry* the Sixth's time they found the inconvenience, fo one Parliament made a Law, that only he that had forty Shillings *per annum* fhould give his voice, they under fhould be excluded. They made the Law who had the voice of all, as well under forty Shillings as above; and thus it continues at this day. All confent civilly to a Parliament, Women are involv'd in the Men, Children in thofe of perfect age, thofe that are under forty Shillings a-year, in thofe that have forty Shillings a-year, thofe of forty Shillings in the Knights.

2. All things are brought to the Parliament, little to the Courts of Juftice; juft as in a room where there is a Banquet prefented, if there be Perfons of Quality there, the People muft expect, and ftay till the great ones have done.

3. The Parliament flying upon feveral Men, and then letting them alone, does as a Hawk that flyes a Covey of Partridges, and when fhe has flown them a great way, grows weary and takes a Tree; then the Faulconer lures her down, and takes her to his fift: on they go again, *hei rett*, up springs another Covey, away

goes the Hawk, and as she did before, takes another Tree. &c.

4. Diffenters in Parliament may at length come to a good end, tho' firſt there be a great deal of do, and a great deal of noiſe, which mad wild
as in brewing of Wreſt-Beer, there's a great deal of buſineſs in grinding the Mault, and that ſpoils any Mans cloaths that comes near it; then it muſt be maſh'd, then comes a Fellow in and drinks Wort, and he's drunk, then they keep a huge quarter when they carry it into the Cellar, and a twelve month after 'tis delicate fine Beer.

5. It muſt neceſſarily be that our Diſtempers are worſe than they were in the beginning of the Parliament. If a Phiſician comes to a ſick Man, he him blood, it may be ſcarifyes him, cups him, puts him into a great diforder, before he makes him well; and if he be ſent for to cure an Ague, and he finds his Patient hath many diſeaſes, a Dropſie, and a Palſie applies remedies to 'em all, which makes the cure longer and the dearer: this is the caſe.

6. The Parliament-men are as great Princes as in the World, when whatſoever they pleaſe is Priviledge of Parliament; no man muſt know the number of their Priviledges, and whatſoever they diſlike is breach of Priviledge. The Duke of *Venice* is no more than Speaker of the Houſe of Commons; but the Senate at *Venice*, are not ſo much as our Parliament-men, nor have they that power over the People, who yet exerciſe the greateſt Tyranny that is anywhere. In plain truth, breach of Priviledge is only the actual taking away of a Member of the Houſe, the reſt are Offences againſt the Houſe. For example, to take out Proceſs againſt a Parliament-man, or the like.

7. The Parliament-party, if the Law be for them, they call for the Law; if it be againſt them, they will go to a Parliamentary way; if no Law be for them, then for Law again: Like him that firſt call'd for Sack to heat him, then ſmall Drink to cool his Sack, then Sack again to

Penance.

1. Penance is only the Punishment inflicted, not Penitence, which is the right word; a man comes not to do Penance, because he repents him of his Sin, but because he is compell'd to it; he curses him, and could kill him that sends him thither. The old Canons wisely enjoyn'd three years Penance, sometimes more, because in that time a man got a habit of Vertue, and so committed that sin no more, for which he did Penance.

People.

1. There is not any thing in the World more abus'd than this Sentence, *Salus populi suprema Lex esto*, for we apply it, as if we ought to forsake the known Law, when it may be most for the advantage of the people, when it means no such thing. For first, 'tis not *Salus populi suprema Lex est*, but *esto*, it being one of the Laws of the twelve Tables, and after divers Laws made, some for Punishment, some for Reward, then follows this, *Salus populi suprema Lex esto*: that is, in all the Laws you make, have a special eye to the good of the people, and then what does this concern the way they now go?

2. *Objection*, He that makes one, is greater than he that is made; the People make the King, *ergo*, &c.

Answ. This does not hold, for if I have 1000*l.* per Annum, and give it you and leave my self ne're a penny, I made you, but when you have my Land, you are greater than I. The Parish makes the Constable, and when the Constable is made, he governs the Parish. The answer to all these Doubts is, Have you agreed so? if you have, then it must remain till you have alter'd it.

Pleasure.

1. Pleasure is nothing else but the intermission of pain, the enjoying of some thing I am in great trouble for 'till I have it.

2. 'Tis a wrong way to proportion other mens pleasures to our selves; 'tis like a Child's using a little Bird [O poor Bird thou shalt sleep with me] so lays it in his Bosome, and stifles it with his hot breath, the Bird had

rather be in the cold Air: And yet too 'tis the moſt pleaſing flattery, to like what other men like.

3. 'Tis moſt undoubtedly true, that all men are equally given to their pleaſure, only thus, one mans pleaſure lyes one way, and anothers another. Pleaſures are all alike, ſimply conſidered in themſelves, he that hunts, or he that governs the Common-wealth, they both pleaſe themſelves alike, only we commend that, whereby we our ſelves receive ſome benefit. As if a man place his delight in things that tend to the common good, he that takes pleaſure to hear Sermons, enjoys himſelf as much as he that hears Plays, and could he that loves Plays endeavour to love Sermons, poſſibly he might bring himſelf to it as well as to any other Pleaſure. At firſt it may ſeem harſh and tedious, but afterwards 'twould be pleaſing and delightful. So it falls out in that, which is the great pleaſure of ſome men, Tobacco, at firſt they could not abide it, and now they cannot be without it.

4. Whilſt you are upon Earth enjoy the good things that are here (to that end were they given) and be not melancholly, and wiſh yourſelf in Heaven. If a King ſhould give you the keeping of a Caſtle, with all things belonging to it, Orchards, Gardens, &c., and bid you uſe them; withal promiſe you that after twenty years to remove you to Court, and to make you a Privy Councellor. If you ſhould neglect your Caſtle, and refuſe to eat of thoſe fruits, and ſit down, and whine, and wiſh you were a Privy Councellor, do you think the King would be pleaſed with you?

5. Pleaſures of Meat, Drink, Cloaths, &c., are forbidden thoſe that know not how to uſe them, just as Nurſes cry pah! when they ſee a Knife in a Childs hand, they will never ſay any thing to a man.

Philosophy.

1. WHen Men comfort themſelves with Philoſophy, 'tis not becauſe they have got two or three Sentences, but becauſe they have digeſted thoſe Sentences, and made them their own: So upon the matter, Philoſophy is nothing but Diſcretion.

Poetry.

1. *Ovid* was not only a fine Poet, but [as a man may speak] a great Canon Lawyer, as appears in his *Fasti*, where we have more of the Festivals of the Old *Romans* than any where else: 'tis pity the rest are lost.

2. There is no reason Plays should be in Verse, either in Blank or Rhime, only the Poet has to say for himself, that he makes something like that, which some body made before him. The old Poets had no other reason but this, their Verse was sung to Musick, otherwise it had been a senseless thing to have fetter'd up themselves.

3. I never Converted but two, the one was Mr. *Crasham* from writing against Plays, by telling him a way how to understand that place [of putting on Womens Apparel] which has nothing to do in the business [as neither has it, that the Fathers speak against Plays in their time, with reason enough, for they had real Idolatries mix'd with their Plays, having three Altars perpetually upon the Stage.] The other was a Doctor of Divinity, from preaching against Painting, which simply in it self is no more hurtful, than putting on my Cloaths, or doing any thing to make my self like other folks, that I may not be odious nor offensive to the Company. Indeed if I do it with an ill intention, it alters the Case, so if I put on my Gloves with an intention to do a mischief, I am a Villain.

4. 'Tis a fine thing for Children to learn to make Verse, but when they come to be men they must speak like other men, or else they will be laught at. 'Tis Ridiculous to speak, or write, or preach in Verse. As 'tis good to learn to dance, a man may learn his Leg, learn to go handsomly, but 'tis ridiculous for him to dance, when he should go.

5. 'Tis ridiculous for a Lord to Print Verses, 'tis well enough to make them to please himself, but to make them publick, is foolish. If a man in his private Chamber twirls his Bandstrings, or plays with a Rush

to please himself, 'tis well enough, but if he should go into *Fleet street*, and sit upon a Stall, and twirl a Bandstring, or play with a Rush, then all the Boys in the

6. Verse proves nothing but the quantity of Syllables, they are not meant for Logick.

Pope.

1. A Popes Bull and a Popes Brief differ very much, as with us the great Seal and the Privy Seal. The Bull being the higheſt Authority the King can give, the Brief is of leſs. The Bull has a Leaden Seal upon silk, hanging upon the Inſtrument. The Brief has *sub Annulo Piscatoris* upon the side.

2. He was a wise Pope, that when one that used to be merry with him, before he was advanc't to the Popedom, refrain'd afterwards to come at him, (presuming he was busie in governing the Christian World) the Pope sends for him, bids him come again, and (says he) we will be merry as we were before, for thou little thinkest what a little Foolery governs the whole World.

3. The Pope in sending Rellicks to Princes, does as Wenches do by their *Waſſals* at *New-years-tide*, they present you with a Cup, and you must drink of a flabby stuff; but the meaning is, that you must Moneys, ten times more than it is worth.

4. The Pope is Infallible, where he hath power to command, that is where he must be obey'd, so is every Supream Power and Prince. They that stretch his Infallibility further, do they know not what.

5. When a Proteſtant and a Papiſt Diſpute, they talk like two Madmen, becauſe they do not agree their Principles, the one way is to deſtroy the Popes Power, for if he hath Power to command me, 'tis not my alledging Reaſons to the contrary can keep me from obeying: For Example, if a Conſtable command me to wear a Green Suit to morrow, and has power to *make me*, 'tis not my alledging a hundred Reaſons of *the Folly* of it can excuſe me from doing it.

6. There was a time when the Pope had Power here in *England*, and there was excellent ufe made of it, for 'twas only to ferve turns, (as might be manifefted out of the Records of the Kingdom, which Divines know little of.) If the King did not like what the Pope would have, he would forbid the Pope's Legate to land upon his ground. So that the Power was truly then in the King, though fuffer'd in the Pope. But now the Temporal and the Spiritual Power (Spiritual fo call'd becaufe ordain'd to a Spiritual end) fpring both from one Fountain, they are like to twift that.

7. The Proteftants in *France* bear Office in the State, becaufe though their Religion be different, yet they acknowledge no other King but the King of *France*. The Papifts in *England* they muft have a King of their own, a Pope, that muft do fomething in our Kingdom, therefore there is no reafon they fhould enjoy the fame Priviledges.

8. *Amfterdam* admits of all Religions but Papifts, and 'tis upon the fame Account. The Papifts where e're they live, have another King at *Rome*; all other Religions are fubject to the prefent State, and have no Prince elfe-where.

9. The Papifts call our Religion a Parliamentary Religion, but there was once, I am fure, a Parliamentary Pope. Pope *Urban* was made Pope in *England* by Act of Parliament, againft *Pope Clement*; the Act is not in the Book of Statutes, either becaufe he that compiled the Book, would not have the Name of the Pope there, or elfe he would not let it appear that they medled with any fuch thing, but 'tis upon the Rolls.

10. When our Clergy preach againft the Pope, and the Church of *Rome*, they preach againft themfelves, and crying down their Pride, their Power, and their Riches, have made themfelves poor and contemptible enough, they dedicate firft to pleafe their Prince, not confidering what would follow. Juft as if a man were to go a Journey, and feeing at his firft fetting out the way clean and fair, ventures forth in his Slippers, not confidering the Dirt and the Sloughs are a little further off, or how fuddenly the Weather may change.

Popery.

1. THE demanding a Noble, for a dead body paffing through a Town, came from hence in time of Popery, they carry'd the dead body into the Church, where the Prieft faid Dirgies, and twenty Dirgies at fourpence a piece comes to a Noble, but now 'tis forbidden by an Order from my Lord Marfhal, the Heralds carry his Warrant about them.

2. We charge the Prelatical Clergy with Popery to make them odious, though we know they are guilty of no fuch thing: Juft as heretofore they call'd Images Mammets, and the Adoration of Images Mammettry: that is, *Mahomet* and *Mahometry*, odious names, when all the World knows the *Turks* are forbidden Images by their Religion.

Power, State.

1. THere is no ftretching of Power, 'tis a good rule, eat within your Stomack, act within your Commiffion.

2. They that govern moft make leaft noife. You fee when they row in a Barge, they that do drudgery-work, flafh, and puff, and fwear, but he that governs, fits quietly at the Stern, and fcarce is feen to ftir.

3. Syllables govern the world.

4. [*All Power is of God*] means no more than *Fides eft fervanda.* When St. *Paul* faid this, the people had made *Nero* Emperour. They agree, he to command, they to obey. Then God comes in, and cafts a hook upon them, keep your Faith, then comes in, all power is of God. Never King dropt out of the Clouds. God did not make a new Emperour, as the King makes a Juftice of peace.

5. Chrift himfelf was a great obferver of the Civil power, and did many things only juftifiable, becaufe the State requir'd it, which were things meerly Temporary for the time that State ftood. But Divines make ufe of them to gain power to themfelves, (as for example) that of *Dic Ecclefiæ*, tell the Church; there was then a Sanhedrim, a Court to tell it to, and therefore they would have it fo now.

6. Divines ought to do no more than what the permits. Before the State became they made their own Laws, and thofe that did not obferve them, they Excommunicated, [*naughty men*] they fuffer'd them to come no more amongft them. But if they would come amongft them, how could they hinder them? By what Law? by what Power? they were ftill fubject to the State, which was Heathen. Nothing better expreffes the condition of Chriftians in thofe times, than one of the Meetings you have in *London*, of men of the fame Country, of *Suffex*-men, or *Bedfordfhire*-men, they appoint their meeting, and they agree, and make Laws amongft themfelves [*He that is not there fhall pay double, &c.*] and if any one misbehave himfelf, they fhut him out of their Company; but can they recover a Forfeiture made concerning their meeting by any Law? Have they any power to compel one to pay? but afterwards when the State became Chriftian, all the power was in them, and they gave the Church as much, or as little as they pleas'd, and took away when they pleas'd, and added

7. The Church is not only Subject to the Civil Power with us that are Proteftants, but alfo in *Spain*, if the Church does Excommunicate a man for what it fhould not, the Civil Power will take him out of their hands. So in *France*, the Bifhop of *Angiers* alter'd fomething in the Breviary, they complain'd to the Parliament at *Paris*, they made him alter it again, with a [*comme abufe*].

8. The Parliament of *England* has no Arbitrary Power in point of Judicature, but in point of making Law only.

9. If the Prince be *fervus natura*, of a fervile bafe Spirit, and the Subjects *liberi*, Free and Ingenuous, oft-times they depofe their Prince, and govern themfelves. On the contrary, if the people be *Servi Natura*, and fome one amongft them of a Free and Ingenuous Spirit, he makes himfelf King of the reft, and this is the Caufe of all Changes in State, Common-wealths into Monarchies, and Monarchies into Common-wealths.

10. In a troubled State we muſt do as in-foul Weather upon the *Thames*, not think to cut directly through, fo the Boat may be quickly full of water, but rife and fall as the Waves do, give as much as conveniently we can.

Prayer.

1. IF I were a Miniſter, I ſhould think my felf moſt in my Office, Reading of Prayers, and Difpenſing the Sacraments; and 'tis ill done to put one to Officiate in the Church, whoſe Perſon is contemptible out of it. Should a great Lady, that was invited to be a Goſſip, in her place fend her Kitchen-Maid, 'twould be ill taken, yet ſhe is a Woman as well as ſhe, let her fend her Woman at leaſt.

2. [*You ſhall pray*] is the right way, becauſe according as the Church is fettled, no man may make a Prayer in Publick of his own head.

3. 'Tis not the Original Common-Prayer-Book, why, ſhew me an Original Bible, or an Original *Magna Charta*.

4. Admit the Preacher prays by the Spirit, yet that very Prayer is Common-Prayer to the People; they are ty'd as much to his words, as in faying [*Almighty and moſt merciful Father*] is it then unlawful in the Miniſter, but not unlawful in the People?

5. There are fome Mathematicians, that could with one fetch of their Pen make an exact Circle, and with the next touch point out the Centre, is it therefore reaſonable to haniſh all ufe of the Compaſſes? Set Forms are a pair of Compaſſes.

6. [*God hath given gifts unto men*] General Texts prove nothing: let him ſhew me *John*, *William* or *Thomas* in the Text, and then I will believe him. If a man hath a voluble Tongue, we fay, He hath the gift of Prayer. His gift is to pray long, that I fee; but does he pray better?

7. We take care what we fpeak to men, but to God we may fay any thing.

8. The People muſt not think a thought towards *God, but as* their Paſtours will put it into their *Mouths:* they will make right Sheep of us.

9. The *English* Priests would do that in English which the *Romish* do in Latin, keep the people in Ignorance; but some of the people out-do them at their own Game.

10. Prayer should be short, without giving God Almighty Reasons why he should grant this, or that, he knows best what is good for us. should ask you a Suit of Cloaths, and give you Reasons (otherwise he cannot wait upon you, he cannot go abroad but he shall discredit you) would you endure it? you know it better than he, let him ask a Suit of Cloaths.

11. If a Servant that has been fed with good Beef, goes into that part of *England*, where Salmon is first he is pleas'd with his Salmon, and Beef, but after he has been there a while, he grows weary of his Salmon, and wishes for his good Beef again. We have a while been much taken this praying by the Spirit, but in time we may weary of it, and wish for our *Common-Prayer*.

'Tis hop'd we may be cur'd of our Extempory Prayers the same way the Grocer's-Boy is cur'd of his eating Plumbs, when we have had our Belly full

Preaching.

1. Othing is more mistaken than that Speech [*Preach the Gospel*] for 'tis not to make long Harangues, as they do now a-days, but to tell the news of Christs coming into the World, and when that is done, or where 'tis known Preacher's work is done.

2. Preaching in the first sence of the word ceas'd as soon as ever the Gospels were written.

3. When the Preacher says, this is the meaning of the Holy Ghost in such a place, in sense he can mean no more than this, that is, I by studdying of the place, by comparing one place with another, by weighing what goes before, and what comes after, think this is the meaning of the Holy Ghost, and for shortness of Expression I say, the Holy Ghost says thus, or this is the meaning of the Spirit of God. So the Judge speaks of the King's Proclamation, this is

the intention of the King, not that the King had declared his intention any other way to the Judge, but the Judge examining the Contents of the Proclamation, gathers by the Purport of the words, the King's Intention, and then for ſhortneſs of expreſſion ſays, this is the King's Intention.

4. Nothing is Text but what was ſpoken in the Bible, and meant there for Perſon and Place, the reſt is Application, which a diſcreet Man may do well; but 'tis his Scripture, not the Holy Ghoſt.

5. Preaching by the Spirit (as they call it) is moſt eſteem'd by the Common people, becauſe they cannot abide Art or Learning, which they have not been bred up in. Juſt as in the buſineſs of Fencing; if one Country-Fellow amongſt the reſt, has been at the School, the reſt will undervalue his Skill, or tell him he wants Valour. *You come with your School-Tricks: There's* Dick Butcher *has ten times more Mettle in him:* So they ſay to the Preachers, *You come with your School Learning: There's ſuch a one has the Spirit.*

6. The tone in Preaching does much in working upon the Peoples Affections. If a Man ſhould make love in an ordinary Tone, his Miſtreſs would not regard him; and therefore he muſt whine. If a Man ſhould cry Fire, or Murther in an ordinary Voice, no body would come out to help him.

7. Preachers will bring anything into the Text. The Young Maſters of Arts preached againſt Non-Reſidency in the Univerſity, whereupon the Heads made an Order, That no Man ſhould meddle with any thing but what was in the Text. The next Day one preach'd upon theſe Words, *Abraham begat Iſaac;* when he had gone a good way, at laſt he obſerv'd, that *Abraham* was Reſident, for if he had been Non-Reſident, he could never have begat *Iſaac;* and ſo fell foul upon the Non-Reſidents.

8. I could never tell what often Preaching meant, after a Church is ſetled, and we know what is to be done; 'tis juſt as if a Husbandman ſhould once tell his *Servants* what they are to do, when to Sow, when to *Reap,* and afterwards one ſhould come and tell them

twice or thrice a Day what they know already. You muſt Sow your Wheat in *October*, you muſt Reap your Wheat in *Auguſt, &c.*

9. The main Argument why they would have two Sermons a day, is, becauſe they have two Meals a Day; the Soul muſt be fed as well as the Body. But I may as well argue, I ought to have two Noſes, becauſe I have two Eyes, or two Mouths, becauſe I have two Ears. What have Meals and Sermons to do one with another?

10. The Things between God and Man are but few, and thoſe, forſooth, we muſt be told often of; but things between Man and Man are many; thoſe I hear not of above twice a Year, at the Aſſizes, or once a Quarter at the Seſſions; but few come then; nor does the Miniſter exhort the People to go at theſe times to learn their Duty towards their Neighbour. Often Preaching is ſure to keep the Miniſter in Countenance, that he may have ſomething to do.

11. In Preaching they ſay more to raiſe men to love Vertue than men can poſſibly perform, to make them do their beſt; as if you would teach a man to throw the Bar, or make him put out his Strength, you bid him throw further than it is poſſible for him, or any man elſe? Throw over yonder Houſe.

12. In Preaching they do by men as Writers of Romances do by their Chief Knights, bring them into many Dangers, but ſtill fetch them off: So they put men in fear of Hell, but at laſt they bring them to Heaven.

13. Preachers ſay, Do as I ſay, not as I do. But if a Phyſician had the ſame Diſeaſe upon him that I have, and he ſhould bid me do one thing, and he do quite another, could I believe him?

14. Preaching the ſame Sermon to all ſorts of People, is, as if a School-Maſter ſhould read the ſame Leſſon to his ſeveral Formes: If he reads *Amo, amas, amavi*, the higheſt Forms Laugh at him; the younger Boys admire him: So 'tis in preaching to a mix'd Auditory. *Obj.* But it cannot be otherwiſe, the Pariſh cannot be divided into ſeveral Formes: What muſt the

Preacher then do in Discretion? *Answ.* Why then let him use some expressions by which this or that condition of people may know such Doctrine does more especially concern them, it being so delivered that the wisest may be content to hear. For if he delivers it all together, and leaves it to them to single out what belongs to themselves (which is the usual way) 'tis as if a man would bestow Gifts upon Children of several ages: Two years old, four years old, ten years old, *&c.*, and there he brings Tops, Pins, Points, Ribbands, and casts them all in a heap together upon a Table before them: though the Boy of ten years old knows how to chuse his Top, yet the Child of two years old, that should have a Ribband, takes a Pin, and the Pin ere he be aware pricks his Fingers, and then all's out of order, *&c.* Preaching for the most part is the glory of the preacher, to show himself a fine man. Catechising would do much better.

15. Use the best Arguments to perswade, though but few understand, for the ignorant will sooner believe the judicious of the Parish, than the Preacher himself, and they teach when they dissipate what he has said, and believe it the sooner confirm'd by men of their own side. For betwixt the Laity and the Clergy, there is, as it were, a continual driving of a bargain; something the Clergy would still have us be at, and therefore many things are heard from the Preacher with suspicion. They are affraid of some ends, which are easily assented to, when they have it from some of themselves. 'Tis with a Sermon as 'tis with a Play; many come to see it, which do not understand it; and yet hearing it cry'd up by one, whose judgment they cast themselves upon, and of power with them, they swear and will die in it, that 'tis a very good Play, which they would not have done if the Priest himself had told them so. As in a great School, 'tis the Master that teaches all; the Monitor does a great deal of work; it may be the boys are affraid to see the Master: so in a Parish 'tis not the Minister does all; *the greater* Neighbour teaches the lesser, the Master of *the house teaches* his Servant, *&c.*

16. Firſt in your Sermons uſe your Logick, and then your Rhetorick. Rhetorick without Logick is like a Tree with Leaves and Bloſſoms, but no Root; yet I confeſs more are taken with Rhetorick than Logick, becauſe they are catched with a free Expreſſion, when they underſtand not Reaſon. Logick muſt be natural, or it is worth nothing at all: Your Rhetorick figures may be learn'd; That Rhetorick is beſt which is moſt ſeaſonable and moſt catching. An inſtance we have in that old blunt Commander at *Cadiz*, who ſhew'd himſelf a good Oratour, being to ſay ſomething to his Souldiers (which he was not us'd to do) he made them a Speech to this purpoſe; *What a ſhame will it be, you Engliſhmen, that feed upon good Beef and Breweſs, to let thoſe Raſcally Spaniards beat you, that eat nothing but Oranges and Limons?* And ſo put more Courage into his Men than he could have done with a more learned Oration. Rhetorick is very good, or ſtark naught: There's no *medium* in Rhetorick. If I am not fully perſwaded I laugh at the Oratour.

17. 'Tis good to preach the ſame thing again, for that's the way to have it learn'd. You ſee a Bird by often whiſtling to learn a tune, and a Month after record it to her ſelf.

18. 'Tis a hard caſe a Miniſter ſhould be turned out of his Living for ſomething they inform he ſhould ſay in his Pulpit. We can no more know what a Miniſter ſaid in his Sermon by two or three words pickt out of it, than we can tell what Tune a Muſician play'd laſt upon the Lute, by two or three ſingle Notes.

Predeſtination.

1. They that talk nothing but Predeſtination, and will not proceed in the way of Heaven till they be ſatisfied in that point, do, as a man that would not come to *London*, unleſs at his firſt ſtep he might ſet his foot upon the top of *Paul's*.

2. For a young Divine to begin in his Pulpit with Predeſtination, is as if a man were coming into *London* and at his firſt ſtep would think to ſet his foot, &c.

3. Predeſtination is a point inacceſſible, out of our

reach; we can make no notion of it, 'tis fo full of intricacy, fo full of contradiction : 'tis in good earneft, as we ftate it, half a dozen Bulls one upon another.

4. Doctor *Prideaux* in his Lectures, feveral days us'd Arguments to prove Predeftination ; at laft tells his Auditory they are damn'd that do not believe it; doing herein juft like School-boys, when one of them has got an Apple, or fomething the reft have a mind to, they ufe all the Arguments they can to get fome of it from them: *I gave you fome t'other day: You fhall have fome with me another time:* when they cannot they tell him he's a Jackanapes, a Rogue and a Rafcal.

Preferment.

1. WHen you would have a Child go to fuch a place, and you find him unwilling, you tell him he fhall ride a Cock-horfe, and then he will go prefently : So do thofe that govern the State, deal by men, to work them to their ends ; they tell them they fhall be advanc'd to fuch or fuch a place, and they will do anything they would have them.

2. A great place ftrangely qualifies. *John Read* (was in the right) *Groom of the Chamber to my Lord of* Kent. Attorney *Noy* being dead, fome were faying, How will the King do for a fit man? why, Any man, (fays *John Read*) may execute the Place. I warrant (fays my Lord) thou thinkft thou underftand'ft enough to perform it. Yes, quoth *John*, Let the King make me Attorney, and I would fain fee that man, that tell me, there's any thing I underftand not.

3. When the Pageants are a coming there's a thrufting and a riding upon one another's backs, to look out at the Window ; ftay a little and they will come juft to you, you may fee them quietly. So 'tis when a new Statefman or Officer is chofen; there's great expectation and liftning who it fhould be ; ftay a while, and you may know quietly.

4. Miffing Preferment makes the upon the Bifhops : Men that are in hopes and in *way of rifing,* keep in the Channel, but they that have none, feek new ways : 'Tis fo amongft the Lawyers;

he that hath the Judges Ear, will be very obfervant of the way of the Court; but he that hath no regard will

5. My Lord *Digby* having fpoken fomething in the Houfe of Commons, for which they would have queftion'd him, was prefently called to the Upper Houfe. He did by the Parliament as an Ape when he hath done fome waggery; his Mafter fpies him, and he looks for his Whip, but before he can come at him, whip fays he to the top of the houfe.

6. Some of the Parliament were difcontented, that they wanted places at Court, which others had got; but when they had them once, then they were quiet. Juft as at a Chriftning fome that get no Sugar Plums, when the reft have, mutter and grumble; prefently the Wench comes again with her Basket of Sugar Plums, and then they catch and fcramble and when they have got them, you hear no more of them.

𝔓𝔯æ𝔪𝔲𝔫𝔦𝔯𝔢.

1. Here can be no *Præmunire*. A *Præmunire* (fo call'd from the word *Præmunire facias*) was when a man laid an Action in an Ecclefiaftical Court, for which he could have no remedy in any of the King's Courts; that is in the Courts of Common Law, by reafon the Ecclefiaftical Courts before *Henry* the Eight were fubordinate to the Pope, and fo it was *Contra coronam et dignitatem Regis;* but now the Ecclefiaftical Courts are equally fubordinate t King. Therefore it cannot be *contra coronam tatem Regis*, and fo no *Præmunire*.

𝔓𝔯𝔢𝔯𝔬𝔤𝔞𝔱𝔦𝔳𝔢.

1. Rerogative is fomething that can be told what it is, not fomething that has no name. Juft as you fee the Archbifhop his Prerogative Court, but we know what is done in that Court. So the King's Prerogative is not his will; or what Divines make it, a Power to do what he lifts.

2. The King's Prerogative, that is, the King's Law.

For example, if you ask whether a Patron may present to a Living after six months by Law? I answer no. If you ask whether the King may? I answer he may by his Prerogative, that is by the Law that concerns him in that case.

Presbytery.

1. They that would bring in a new Government, would very fain perswade us, they meet it in Antiquity; thus they interpret Presbyters, when they meet the word in the Fathers; Other professions likewise pretend to Antiquity. The Alchymist will find his Art in *Virgil*'s *Aureus ramus*, and he that delights in Opticks will find them in *Tacitus*. When *Cæsar* came into *England* they would perswade us, they had perspective-Glasses, by which he could discover what they were doing upon the Land, because it is said, *Positio Speculis;* the meaning is, His Watch, or his Sentinel discover'd this, and this unto him.

2. Presbyters have the greatest power of any Clergy in the World, and gull the Laity most; for example; Admit there be twelve Laymen to six Presbyters, the six shall govern the rest as they please. First because they are constant, and the others came in like Church-Wardens in their turns, which is an huge advantage. Men will give way to them who have been in place before them. Next the Laymen have other professions to follow; the Presbyters make it their sole business; and besides too they learn and study the Art of perswading; some of *Geneva* have confess'd as much.

3. The Presbyter with his Elders about him is like a young Tree fenc'd about with two or three or four Stakes; the Stakes defend it, and hold it up; but the Tree only prospers and flourishes; it may be some Willow stake may bear a Leaf or two, but it comes to nothing. Lay-Elders are Stakes, the Presbyter the Tree that flourishes.

4. When the Queries were sent to the Assembly concerning the *Jus Divinum* of Presbytery; their asking time to answer them, was a Satyr upon themselves. For if it were to be seen in the Text, they might quickly turn to the place, and shew us it. Their

delaying to Anfwer makes us think there's no fuch thing there. They do juft as you have feen a fellow do at a Tavern Reckoning, when he fhould come to pay his Reckoning he puts his hands in his Pockets, and keeps a grabling and a fumbling, and fhaking, at laft tells you he has left his Money at home; when all the company knew at firft, he had no Money there, for every man can quickly find his own Money.

Priests of Rome.

1. THe reafon of the Statute againft Priefts, was this; In the beginning of Queen *Elizabeth* there was a Statute made, that he that drew men from their Civil obedience was a Traitor. It happen'd this was done in Privacies and Confeffions, when there could be no proof; therefore they made another Act, that for a Prieft to be in *England*, was Treafon, becaufe they prefum'd that was his bufinefs to fetch men off from their Obedience.

2. When Queen *Elisabeth* dy'd, and King *James* came in, an Irifh Prieft does thus exprefs it; *Elisabetha in orcum detrufa, fucceffit Jacobus, alter Hæreticus.* You will afk why they did ufe fuch Language in their Church. *Anfw.* Why does the Nurfe tell the Child of Raw-head and Bloudy-bones, to keep it in awe?

3. The Queen-Mother and Count *Roffet*, are to the Priefts and Jefuits like the honey-pot to the Flies.

4. The Priefts of *Rome* aim but at two things, To get power from the King, and Money from the Subject.

5. When the Priefts come into a Family, they do as a man that would fet fire on a houfe; he does not put fire to the Brick-wall, but thrufts it into the Thatch. They work upon the women, and let the men alone.

6. For a Prieft to turn a man when he lies a-dying, is juft like one that hath a long time folicited a woman, and cannot obtain his end; at length makes her drunk, and fo lies with her.

Prophecies.

1. DReams and Prophecies do thus much good; They make a man go on with boldnefs and courage, upon a Danger or a Miftrefs; if

he obtains, he attributes much to them; if he miscarries, he thinks no more of them, or is no more thought of himself.

Proverbs.

1. THE Proverbs of several Nati studied by Bishop *Andrews*, and the reason he gave, was, Because by them he knew the minds of several Nations which is a brave thing; as we count him a wise man, that knows the minds and insides of men, which is done by knowing what is habitual to them. Proverbs are habitual to a Nation, being transmitted from Father to Son.

Question.

1. WHen a doubt is propounded, you must learn to distinguish, and show wherein a thing holds, and wherein it hold. Ay, or no, never answer'd any Question. The not distinguishing where things should be distinguish'd, and the not confounding, where things should be confounded, is the cause of all the mistakes in the World.

Reason.

1. IN giving Reasons, Men commonly do with us as the Woman does with her Child; when she goes to Market about her business, she tells it she goes to buy it a fine thing, to buy it a Cake or some Plums. They give us such Reasons as they think we will be catched withal, but never let us know the Truth.

2. When the School-men talk of *Recta* Morals, either they understand Reason, as it is govern'd by a Command from above; or else they say no more than a Woman, when she says a thing is so, because it is so; that is her Reason perswades her 'tis so. The other Acception has Sence in it. As take a Law of the Land, I must not depopulate, my Reason tells me so. Why? Because if I do, I incurr the detriment.

3. The Reason of a Thing is not to be enquired after, till you are sure the Thing it self be so. We commonly are at [*What's the Reason of it?*] before we are sure of the Thing. 'Twas an excellent Question of my

Lady *Cotten*, when Sir *Robert Cotten* was magnifying of a Shooe, which was *Mofes*'s or *Noah*'s, and wondring at the ſtrange Shape and Faſhion of it: *But Mr.* Cotten, ſays ſhe, *are you fure it is a Shooe.*

Retaliation.

AN *Eye for an Eye, and a Tooth for a Tooth;* That does not mean, that if I put out another Man's Eye, therefore I muſt loſe one of my own, (for what is he the better for that?) though this be commonly received; but it means, I ſhall give him what Satisfaction an Eye ſhall be judged to be worth.

Reverence.

1. 'TIS ſometimes unreaſonable to look after Reſpect and Reverence, either from a Man's own Servant, or other Inferiours. A great Lord and a Gentleman talking together, there came a Boy by, leading a Calf with both his hands; ſays the Lord to the Gentleman, You ſhall ſee me make the Boy let go his Calf; with that he came towards him, thinking the Boy would have put off his Hat, but the Boy took no Notice of him. The Lord ſeeing that, *Sirrah*, ſays he, *Do you not know me that you uſe no Reverence?* Yes, ſays the Boy, *if your Lordſhip will hold my Calf, I will put off my Hat.*

Non-Reſidency.

1. THE People thought they had a great Victory over the Clergy, when in *Henry* the Eighth's time they got their Bill paſſed, That a Clergy-man ſhould have but Two Livings; before a Man might have Twenty or Thirty; 'twas but getting a Diſpenſation from the Pope's Limiter, or Gatherer of the *Peter-Pence*, which was eaſily got, as now you may have a *Licence* to eat Fleſh.

2. As ſoon as a Miniſter is made, he hath Power to Preach all over the World, but the Civil-Power reſtrains him; he cannot preach in this Pariſh, or in that; there is one already appointed. Now if the State allows him Two Livings, then he hath Two Places where he may Exerciſe his Function, and ſo has the more Power

to do his Office, which he might do every where if he were not restrained.

Religion.

1. KIng *James* said to the Fly, Have I Three Kingdoms, and thou must needs fly into my Eye? Is there not enough to meddle with upon the Stage, or in Love, or at the Table, but Religion?

2. Religion amongst Men appears to me like the Learning they got at School. Some Men forget all they learned, others spend upon the Stock, and some improve it. So some Men forget all the Religion that was taught them when they were Young, others spend upon that stock, and some improve it.

3. Religion is like the Fashion, one Man wears his Doublet slash'd, another lac'd, another plain; but every Man has a Doublet: So every Man has his Religion. We differ about Trimming.

4. Men say they are of the same Religion for Quietness sake; but if the matter were well Examin'd you would scarce find Three any where of the same Religion in all Points.

5. Every Religion is a getting Religion; for though I myself get nothing, I am Subordinate to those that do. So you may find a Lawyer in the *Temple* that gets little for the present, but he is fitting himself to be in time one of those great Ones that do get.

6. Alteration of Religion is dangerous, because we know not where it will stay; 'tis like a *Milstone* that lies upon the top of a pair of Stairs, 'tis hard to remove it, but if once it be thrust off the first Stair, it never stays till it comes to the bottom.

7. *Question*. Whether is the Church or the Scripture Judge of Religion? *Answer*. In truth neither, but the State. I am troubled with a Boil; I call a Company of Chirurgeons about me; one prescribes one thing, another another; I single out something I like, and ask you that stand by, and are no Chirurgeons, what you think of it: You like it too; you and I are Judges of *the* Plaster, and we bid them prepare it, and there's an end. Thus 'tis in Religion; the Protestants say they

will be judged by the Scripture; the Papifts fay fo too; but that cannot fpeak. A Judge is no Judge, except he can both fpeak and command Execution; but the truth is they never intend to agree. No doubt the Pope where he is Supream, is to be Judge; if he fay we in *England* ought to be fubject to him, then he muft draw his Sword and make it good.

8. By the Law was the Manual received into the Church before the Reformation, not by the Civil Law, that had nothing to do in it; nor hy the Canon Law, for that Manual that was here, was not in *France*, nor in *Spain*; but by Cuftom, which is the Common Law of *England*; and Cuftom is but the Elder Brother to a Parliament: and fo it will fall out to be nothing that the Papifts fay, Ours is a Parliamentary Religion, by reafon the Service-Book was Eftablifhed by Act of Parliament, and never any Service-Book was fo before. That will be nothing that the Pope fent the Manual: 'Twas ours, becaufe the State received it. The State ftill makes the Religion and receives into it, what will beft agree with it. Why are the *Venetians* Roman Catholicks? Because the State likes the Religion: All the World knows they care not Three Pence for the Pope. The Council of *Trent* is not at this day admitted in *France*.

9. *Papift*. Where was your Religion before *Luther*, an Hundred Years ago? *Proteftant*. Where was *America* an Hundred or Sixfcore years ago? Our Religion was where the reft of the Chriftian Church was. *Papift*. Our Religion continued ever fince the Apoftles, and therefore 'tis better. *Proteftant*. So did ours. That there was an interruption of it, will fall out to be nothing, no more than if another Earl fhould tell me of the Earl of *Kent*, faying, He is a better Earl than he, becaufe there was one or two of the Family of *Kent* did not take the Title upon them: yet all that while they were really Earls; and afterwards a Great Prince declar'd them to be Earls of *Kent*, as he that made the other Family an Earl.

10. Difputes in Religion will never be ended, becaufe there wants a Meafure by which the Bufinefs

would be decided: The *Puritan* would be judged by the Word of God: If he would fpeak clearly, he means himfelf, but he is afhamed to fay fo; and he would have me believe him before a whole Church, that has read the Word of God as well as he. One fays one thing, and another another; and there is, I fay, no Meafure to end the Controverfie. 'Tis juft as if
at Bowls, and both judg'd by the Eye; One fays 'tis his Caft, the other fays 'tis my Caft; and having no Meafure, the Difference is Eternal.
Satyrically exprefs'd the vain Difputes of Divines by *Inigo Lanthorne*, difputing with his Puppet in
Fair: It is fo; It is not fo; It is fo; It
thus one to another a quarter of an Hour together.

11. In Matters of Religion to be rul'd by one that writes againft his Adverfary, and throws all the Dirt he can in his Face, is, as if in point of good Manners a Man fhould be govern'd by one whom he fees at Cuffs with another, and thereupon thinks himfelf bound to give the next Man he meets a Box on the Ear.

12. 'Tis to no purpofe to labour to Reconcile Religions, when the Intereft of Princes will not fuffer it. 'Tis well if they could be Reconciled fo far, that they fhould not cut one another's Throats.

13. There's all the Reafon in the World *Divines* fhould not be fuffer'd to go a Hair beyond their Bounds, for fear of breeding Confufion, fince there now be fo many Religions on Foot. The matter was not fo narrowly to be look'd after when there was but one Religion in Chriftendom; the reft would cry him down for an Heretick, and there was no Body to fide with him.

14. We look after Religion as the Butcher did after his Knife, when he had it in his Mouth.

15. Religion is made a Juggler's Paper; now 'tis a Horfe, now 'tis a Lanthorn, now 'tis a Boar, now 'tis a Man. To ferve Ends Religion is turn'd into all Shapes.

16. Pretending Religion and the Law of God, is to fet all things loofe: When a Man has no mind to do fomething he ought to do by his Contract with Man, *then he gets a Text, and Interprets it as he pleafes, and fo thinks to get loofe.*

17. Some Mens pretending Religion, is like the Roaring Boys way of Challenges, [*Their Reputation is It does not stand with the Honour of a Gentleman,*] God knows, they have neither Honour nor Reputation about them.

18. They talk much of fetling Religion; Religion is well enough fetled already, if we would let it alone: ethinks we might look after, &c.

9. If men would say they took Arms for any thing Religion, they might be beaten out of it by Reason; out of that they never can, for they will not believe whatever you say.

0. The very *Arcanum* of pretending Religion in all Wars is, That something may be found out in which all men may have interest. In this the Groom has as much interest as the Lord. Were it for Land, one has One Thousand Acres, and the other but One; he would not venture so far, as he that has a Thousand. But Religion is equal to both. Had all men Land alike, by a *Lex Agraria*, then all men would say they fought for Land.

Sabbath.

1. HY should I think all the Fourth Commandment belongs to me, when all the Fifth does not? What Land will the Lord give me for honouring my Father? It was spoken to the Jews with reference to the Land of *Canaan*; but the meaning is, If I honour my Parents, God will also bless me. We read the Commandments in the Church as we do *David*'s Psalms, not that all there concerns us, but a great deal of them does.

Sacrament.

1. rist suffered *Judas* to take the Communion. Those Ministers that keep the Parishoners from it, because they will not do as they them, revenge rather than reform.

2. No man can tell whether I am fit to receive the Sacrament; for though I were fit the day before, when he examined me; at least appear'd so to him: yet how can he tell what sin I have committed that night, or

the next morning, or what impious Atheiſtical thoughts I may have about me, when I am approaching to the very Table?

Salvation.

1. WE can beſt underſtand the meaning of σωτηρία, Salvation, from the Jews, to whom the Saviour was promiſed. They held that themſelves ſhould have the chief place of happineſs in the other world; but the Gentiles that were good men, ſhould likewiſe have their portion of Bliſs there too. Now by Chriſt the Partition-Wall is broken down, and the Gentiles that believe in him, are admitted to the ſame place of Bliſs with the Jews; and why then ſhould not that portion of Happineſs ſtill remain to them, who do not believe in Chriſt, ſo they be morally good? This is a charitable opinion.

State.

1. IN a troubled State ſave as much for your own as you can. A Dog had been at Market to buy a Shoulder of Mutton; coming home he met two Dogs by the way, that quarrell'd with him; he laid down his Shoulder of Mutton, and fell to fighting with one of them; in the mean time the other Dog fell to eating his Mutton; he ſeeing that, left the Dog he was fighting with, and fell upon him that was eating; then the other Dog fell to eat; when he perceiv'd there was no remedy, but which of them ſoever he fought withal, his Mutton was in danger, he thought he would have as much of it as he could, and thereupon gave over fighting, and fell to eating himſelf.

Superstition.

1. THey that are againſt Superſtition often-times run into it of the wrong ſide. If I will wear all colours but black, then am I Superſtitious in not wearing black.

2. They pretend not to adore the Croſs, becauſe 'tis ſuperſtitious; for my part I will believe them, when I ſee them throw their money out of their Pockets, and *not till* then.

3. *If there be* any Superſtition truly and properly ſo

called, 'tis their obferving the Sabboth after the Jewifh manner.

Subfidies.

1. HEretofore the Parliament was wary what Subfidies they gave to the King, becaufe they had no account, but now they care not how much they give of the Subjects money, becaufe they give it with one hand and receive it with the other; and fo upon the matter give it themfelves. In the meantime what a cafe the Subjects of *England* are in; if the men they have fent to the Parliament misbehave themfelves, they cannot help it, becaufe the Parliament is eternal.

2. A Subfidy was counted the fifth part of a man's Eftate, and fo fifty Subfidies is five and forty times more than a man is worth.

Simony.

1. THe name of Simony was begot in the Canon-Law; the firft Statute againft it was in Queen *Elizabeth*'s time. Since the Reformation Simony has been frequent: One reafon why it was not practifed in time of Popery, was the Pope's provifion; no man was fure to beftow his own Benefice.

Ship-Money.

1. MR. *Noy* brought in Ship-money firft for Maritine Towns, but that was like putting in a little Augur, that afterwards you may put in a greater; he that pulls down the firft Brick, does the main work, afterwards 'tis eafie to pull down the Wall.

2. They that at firft would not pay Ship-money, till 'twas decided, did like brave men (though perhaps they did no good by the Trial), but they that ftand out fince, and fuffer themfelves to be diftrain'd, never queftioning thofe that do it, do pitifully, for fo they only pay twice as much as they fhould.

Synod Affembly.

1. WE have had no National Synod fince the Kingdom hath been fettled, as now it is, only Provincial; and there will be this inconveniency, to call fo many Divines together; 'twill be to put power in their hands, who are too apt to ufurp

it, as if the Laity were bound by their determination. No, let the Laity confult with Divines on all fides, hear what they fay, and make themfelves Mafters of their reafons; as they do by any other profeffion, when they have a difference before them. For example Goldfmiths, they enquire of them, if fuch a Jewel be of fuch a value, and fuch a Stone of fuch a value, hear them, and then being rational men judge themfelves.

2. Why fhould you have a Synod, when you have a Convocation already, which is a Synod? Would you have a fuperfetation of another Synod? The Clergy of *England* when they caft off the Pope, fubmitted themfelves to the Civil Power, and fo have continued; but thefe challenge to be *Jure Divino*, and fo to be above the Civil Power; thefe challenge power to call before their Presbyteries all perfons for all fins directly againft the Law of God, as proved to be fins by neceffary confequence. If you would buy Gloves, fend for a Glover or two, not Glovers-hall; confult with fome Divines, not fend for a Body.

3. There muft be fome Laymen in the Synod, to overlook the Clergy, leaft they fpoil the Civil work; juft as when the good Woman puts a Cat into the Milk-houfe to kill a Moufe, fhe fends her Maid to look after the Cat, leaft the Cat fhould eat up the Cream.

4. In the Ordinance for the Affembly, the Lords and Commons go under the names of learned, godly, and judicious Divines; there is no difference put betwixt them, and the Minifters in the Context.

5. 'Tis not unufual in the Affembly to revoke their Votes, by reafon they make fo much haft, but 'tis will make them fcorn'd. You never heard of a Council revok'd an Act of its own making, they have been wary in that, to keep up their Infallibility; if they did anything they took away the whole Council, and yet we would be thought infallible as any body: 'tis not enough to fay, the Houfe of Commons revoke their Votes, for theirs are but Civil truths which they by agreement create, and uncreate, as they pleafe: But *the* Truths the Synod deals in are Divine, and when *they have* voted a thing, if it be then true, 'twas true

before, not true becaufe they voted it, nor does it ceafe to be true, becaufe they voted otherwife.

in a Synod, or to the Articles of a Synod, is no fuch terrible thing as they make it; becaufe, if I am of a Synod, 'tis agreed, either tacitely or exprefly. That which the Major part determines, the reft are involv'd in; and therefore I fubfcribe, though my own private Opinion be otherwife; and upon the fame Ground, I may without fcruple fubfcribe to what thofe have determin'd, whom I fent, though my private Opinion be otherwife, having refpect to that which is the Ground of all Affemblies, the major part carries it.

Thanksgibing.

1. AT firft we gave Thanks for every Victory as foon as ever 'twas obtained, but fince we we have had many now we can ftay a good while. We are juft like a Child; give him a Plum, he makes his Leg; give him a fecond Plum, he makes Leg: At laft when his Belly is full, he forgets what he ought to do; then his Nurfe, or fome body ftands by him, puts him in mind of his Duty, *Where's your Leg.*

Tythes.

Ythes are more paid in kind in *England*, than in all *Italy* and *France*. In *France* they have had Impropriations a long time; we had none in *England* till *Henry* the Eight.

To make an Impropriation, there was to be the Confent of the Incumbent, the Patron, and the King; then 'twas confirmed by the Pope: Without all this the Pope could make no Impropriation.

Or what if the Pope gave the *Tythes* to any Man, they therefore be taken away? If the Pope gives me a Jewel, will you therefore take it away from me?

Abraham paid Tythes to *Melchizedeck*, what then? Twas very well done of him: It does not follow therefore that I muft pay Tythes, no more than I am bound to imitate any other Action of *Abraham*'s.

5. 'Tis ridiculous to fay the Tythes are God's part, and therefore the Clergy muft have them: Why, fo

they are if the Layman has them. 'Tis as if one of my Lady *Kent*'s Maids fhould be fweeping this Room, and another of them fhould come and take away the Broom, and tell for a Reafon, why fhe fhould part with it: 'Tis my Lady's Broom: As if it were not my Lady's Broom which of them foever had it.

6. They Confulted in *Oxford* where they might find the beft Argument for their Tythes, fetting afide the *Jus Divinum*; they were advis'd to my Hiftory of Tythes; a Book fo much cry'd
merly; (in which, I dare boldly
Arguments for them than are
where:) Upon this, one writ me word, That my Hiftory of Tythes was now become like *Peleus*'s *Hasta*, to Wound and to Heal. I told him in my Anfwer, I thought I could fit him with a better inftance. 'Twas poffible it might undergo the fame Fate, that *Ariftotle*, *Avicen*, and *Averroes* did in *France*, some Five Hundred Years ago; which were Excommunicated by *Stephen* Bifhop of *Paris*, [by that very name, *Excommunicated*,] becaufe that kind of Learning puzled and troubled their Divinity. But finding themfelves at a lofs, fome Forty Years after (which is much about the time fince I writ my Hiftory) were call'd in again, and fo have continued ever fince.

Trade.

1. THere is no Prince in Chriftendom but is directly a Tradefman, though in another way than an ordinary Tradefman. For the purpofe, I have a Man, I bid him lay out Twenty Shillings in fuch Commodities, but I tell him for every Shilling he lays out I will have a Penny. I Trade as well as he. This every Prince does in his Cuftoms.

2. That which a Man is bred up in, he thinks no Cheating; as your Tradefman thinks not fo of his Profeffion, but calls it a Myftery. Whereas if you would teach a Mercer to make his Silks heavier, than what he has been ufed to, he would peradventure think that to be Cheating.

3. Every Tradesman professes to cheat me, that asks for his Commodity twice as much as it is worth.

Tradition.

1. SAY what you will against *Tradition*; we know the Signification of Words by nothing but Tradition. You will say the Scripture was written by the Holy *Spirit*, but do you understand that Language 'twas writ in it? No. Then for Example, take these words, [*In principio erat verbum*] How do you know those words signifie, [*In the beginning was the word*,] but by Tradition, because some Body has told you so?

Transubstantiation.

1. THE Fathers using to speak Rhetorically brought up Transubstantiation: As if because it is commonly said, *Amicus est alter idem*, One should go about to prove a Man and his Friend are all one. That Opinion is only Rhetorick turn'd into Logick.

2. There is no greater Argument (though not us'd) against Transubstantiation, than the Apostles at their first Council, forbidding Blood and Suffocation. Would they forbid Blood, and yet enjoin the eating of Blood too?

3. The best way for a pious Man, is to address himself to the Sacrament with that Reverence and Devotion, as if Christ were really there present.

Traitor.

1. 'TIs not seasonable to call a Man Traitor that has an Army at his Heels. One with an Army is a Gallant man. My Lady *Cotten* was in the right, when she laugh'd at the Duchess of *Richmond* for taking such State upon her, when she could Command no Forces. [*She a Duchess, there's in* Flanders *a Duchess indeed*;] meaning the Arch-Duchess.

Trinity.

1. THE Second Person is made of a piece of Bread by the Papist, the Third Person is made of his own Frenzy, Malice, Ignorance and Folly, by the Roundhead (to all these the

Spirit is intituled,] One the Baker makes, the other the Cobler; and betwixt thofe Two, I think the Firft Perfon is fufficiently abufed.

Truth.

1. THe *Ariftotelians* fay, All Truth is contained in *Ariftotle* in one place or another. *Galilæo* makes *Simplicius* fay fo, but fhows the abfurdity of that Speech, by anfwering, All Truth is contained in a leffer Compafs; viz. In the Alphabet. *Ariftotle* is not blam'd for miftaking fometimes; but *Ariftotelians* for maintaining thofe miftakes. They fhould acknowledge the good they have from him, and leave him when he is in the wrong. There never breath'd that Perfon to whom Mankind was more beholden.

2. The way to find out the Truth is by others miftakings: For if I was to go to fuch a place, and one had gone before me on the Right-hand, and he was out; another had gone on the Left-hand, and he was out; this would direct me to keep the middle way, that peradventure would bring me to the place I defir'd to go.

3. In troubled Water you can fcarce fee your Face; or fee it very little, till the Water be quiet and ftand ftill. So in troubled times you can fee little Truth; when times are quiet and fettled, then Truth appears.

Trial.

1. TRials are by one of thefe three ways; by Confeffion, or by Demurrer, that is, Confeffing the Fact, but denying it to be that, wherewith a Man is charged. For Example, Denying it to be Treason, if a Man be charged with Treafon; or by a Jury.

3. *Ordalium* was a Trial; and was either by going over Nine red hot Plough-Shares, (as in the Cafe of Queen *Emma*, accus'd for lying with the Bifhop of *Winchefter*, over which fhe being led Blindfold; and having pafs'd all her Irons, afk'd when fhe fhould come to her Trial;) or 'twas by taking a red hot Coulter in a Man's hand, and carrying it fo many Steps, and then *cafting it* from him. As foon as this was done the

Hands or the Feet were to be bound up, and certain Charms to be faid, and a day or two after to be open'd; and if the parts were whole, the Party was judg'd to be Innocent; and fo on the contrary.

3. The Rack is us'd no where as in *England*: In other Countries 'tis ufed in *Judicature*, when there is a *Semiplena probatio*, a half Proof againft a Man; then to fee if they can make it full, they Rack him if he will not Confefs. But here in *England* they take a Man and Rack him, I do not know why, nor when; not in time of *Judicature*, but when fome Body bids.

4. Some Men before they come to their Trial, are cozen'd to Confefs upon Examination: Upon this Trick, they are made to believe fome Body has confeffed before them; and then they think it a piece of Honour to be clear and ingenious, and that deftroys them.

University.

1. THE beft Argument why *Oxford* fhould have precedence of *Cambridge* is the Act of Parliament, by which *Oxford* is made a Body; made what it is; and *Cambridge* is made what it is; and in the Act it takes place. Befides *Oxford* has the beft Monuments to fhow.

2. 'Twas well faid of One, hearing of a Hiftory Lecture to be founded in the Univerfity; Would to God, fays he, they would direct a Lecture of Difcretion there, this would do more good there an hundred times.

3. He that comes from the Univerfity to govern the State, before he is acquainted with the Men and Manners of the Place, does juft as if he fhould come into the prefence Chamber all Dirty, with his Boots on, his riding Coat, and his Head all daub'd; They may ferve him well enough in the way, but when he comes to Court, he muft conform to the Place.

Vows.

1. SUppofe a man find by his own inclination he has no mind to marry, may he not then Vow Chaftity? *Anfw.* If he does, what a fine thing hath he done? 'tis as if a man did not love

Cheese; and then he would vow to God Almighty never to eat Cheese. He that Vows can mean no more in sense, than this; To do his utmost endeavour to keep his Vow.

Usury.

1. THE *Jews* were forbidden to take Use one of another; but they were not forbidden to take it of other Nations. That being so, I see no reason, why I may not as well take Use for my Money as Rent for my House. 'Tis a vain thing to say, Money begets not Money; for that no doubt it does.

2. Would it not look odly to a Stranger, that should come into this Land, and hear in our Pulpits Usury preach'd against; and yet the Law allow it? Many men use it; perhaps some Churchmen themselves. No Bishop nor Ecclesiastical Judge, that pretends power to punish other faults, dares punish, or at least does punish any man for doing it.

Pious Uses.

1. THE ground of the Ordinary's taking part of a Man's Estate (who dy'd without a Will) to Pious Uses, was this; To give it some body to pray, that his soul might be deliver'd out of Purgatory, now the pious Uses come into his own Pocket, 'Twas well exprest by *John O Powls* in the Play, who acted the Priest; one that was to be hang'd, being brought to the Ladder, would fain have given something to the Poor; he feels for his Purse, (which *John O Powls* had pickt out of his Pocket before) missing it, crys out, He had lost his Purse; now he intended to have given something to the Poor: *John O Powls* bid him be pacified, for the Poor had it already.

War.

1. DO not under-value an Enemy by whom you have been worsted. When our Countrymen came home from fighting with the *Saracens*, and were beaten by them, they pictured *them* with huge, big, terrible Faces (as you still see the Sign of the *Saracen*'s-head is) when in truth they were

like other men. But this they did to save their own Credits.

2. Martial-Law in general, means nothing but the Martial-Law of this, or that place; with us to be us'd in *Fervore Belli*, in the Face of the Enemy, not in time of Peace; there they can take away neither Limb nor Life. The Commanders need not complain for want of it, because our Ancestors have done Gallant things without it.

3. *Question.* Whether may Subjects take up Arms against their Prince? *Answ.* Concieve it thus; Here lies a Shilling betwixt you and me; Ten Pence of the Shilling is yours, Two Pence is mine: By agreement, I am as much King of my Two Pence, as you of your Ten Pence: If you therefore go about to take away my Two Pence, I will defend it; for there you and I are equal, both Princes.

4. Or thus, Two supream Powers meet; one says to the other, Give me your Land; if you will not, I will take it from you: The other, because he thinks himself too weak to resist him, tells him, Of Nine Parts I will give you Three, so I may quietly enjoy the rest, and I will become your Tributary. Afterwards the Prince comes to exact Six Parts, and leaves but Three; the Contract then is broken, and they are in Parity again.

5. To know what Obedience is due to the Prince, you must look into the Contract betwixt him and his People: as if you would know what Rent is due from the Tenant to the Landlord, you must look into the Lease. When the Contract is broken, and there is no third Person to judge, then the Decision is by Arms. And this is the Case between the Prince and the Subject.

6. *Question.* What Law is there to take up Arms against the Prince, in Case he break his Covenant? *Answ.* Though there be no written Law for it, yet there is Custom; which is the best Law of the Kingdom; for in *England* they have always done it. There is nothing exprest between the King of *England* and the King of *France;* that if either Invades the other's Territory, the other shall take up Arms against him, *and yet they* do it upon such an Occasion.

7. 'Tis all one to be plunder'd by a Troop of Horfe, or to have a Man's Goods taken from him by an Order from the Council-Table. To him that dies, 'tis all one whether it be by a Penny Halter, or a Silk Garter; yet I confefs the Silk Garter pleafes more; and like *Trouts* we love to be tickled to Death.

8. The Souldiers fay they Fight for Honour; when the truth is they have their Honour in their Pocket. And they mean the fame thing that pretend to Fight for Religion. Juft as a Parfon goes to Law with his Parifhioners; he fays, For the Good of his Succeffors, that the Church may not lofe its Right; when the meaning is to get the Tythes into his own Pocket.

9. We Govern this War as an unfkilful Man does a Cafting-Net; if he has not the right trick to caft the Net off his Shoulder, the Leads will pull him into the River. I am afraid we fhall pull our felves into Deftruction.

10. We look after the particulars of a Battle becaufe we live in the very time of War. Where as of Battles paft we hear nothing but the number flain. Juft as for the Death of a Man; When he is fick, we talk how he flept this Night, and that Night; what he eat, and what he drunk: But when he is dead, we only fay, He died of a Fever, or name his Difeafe; and there's an end.

11. *Boccaline* has this paffage of Souldiers, They came to *Apollo* to have their profeffion made the Eighth Liberal Science, which he granted. As foon as it was nois'd up and down, it came to the Butchers, and they defir'd their Profeffion might be made the Ninth: For fay they, the Souldiers have this Honour for the killing of Men; now we kill as well as they; but we kill Beafts for the preferving of Men, and why fhould not we have Honour likewife done to us? *Apollo* could not Anfwer their Reafons, fo he revers'd his Sentence, and made the Souldiers Trade a Myftery, as the Butchers is.

Witches.

1. THE Law againft Witches does not prove there be any; but it punifhes the Malice of thofe people, that ufe fuch means, to take away mens Lives. If one fhould profefs that by turning

his Hat thrice, and crying Buz; he could take away a man's life (though in truth he could do no such thing) yet this were a just Law made by the State, that whosoever should turn his Hat thrice, and cry Buz; with an intention to take away a man's life, shall be put to death.

Wife.

1. HE that hath a handsome Wife, by other men is thought happy; 'tis a pleasure to look upon her, and be in her company; but the Husband is cloy'd with her. We are never content with what we have.

2. You shall see a Monkey sometime, that has been playing up and down the Garden, at length leap up to the top of the Wall, but his Clog hangs a great way below on this side; the Bishop's Wife is like that Monkey's Clog, himself is got up very high, takes place of the Temporal Barons, but his wife comes a great way behind.

3. 'Tis reason a man that will have a Wife should be at the charge of her Trinkets, and pay all the scores she sets on him. He that will keep a Monkey, 'tis fit he should pay for the Glasses he breaks.

Wisedom.

1. A Wise Man should never resolve upon any thing, at least never let the World know his Resolution, for if he cannot arrive at that, he is asham'd. How many things did the King resolve in his Declaration concerning *Scotland*, never to do, and yet did 'em all? A man must do according to accidents and Emergencies.

2. Never tell your Resolution before hand; but when the Cast is thrown, Play it as well as you can to win the Game you are at. 'Tis but folly to study, how to Play Size-ace, when you know not whether you shall throw it or no.

3. Wise Men say nothing in dangerous times. The Lion you know call'd the Sheep, to ask her if his breath smelt; she said, Ay; he bit off her head for a *fool*. He call'd the Wolf and askt him: He said no;

he tore him in pieces for a Flatterer. At last he call'd the Fox and ask'd him; truly he had got a Cold and could not smell. King *James*

Wit.

1. WIT and Wisedom differ; Wit is upon the sudden turn, Wisedom about ends.

2. Nature must be the ground-work of Wit and Art; otherwise whatever is done will prove but Jack-puddings work.

3. Wit must grow like Fingers; if it be taken from others, 'tis like Plums stuck upon Black thornes; they are for a while but they come to nothing.

4. He that will give himself to all manner of ways to get Money may be rich; so he that lets fly all he knows or thinks, may by chance be Satyrically witty. Honesty sometimes keeps a man from growing rich; and Civility from being witty.

5. Women ought not to know their own Wit, because they will still be shewing it, and so spoil it; like a Child that will continually be shewing its fine new Coat, till at length it all bedawbs it with its Pah-hands.

6. Fine Wits destroy themselves with their Plots, in meddling with great affairs of State. They commonly do as the Ape that saw the Gunner put Bullets in the Cannon, and was pleas'd with it, and he would be doing so too; at last he puts himself into the Piece, and so both Ape, and Bullet were shot away together.

Women.

1. LET the Women have power of their heads, *because of the Angels*. The reason of the words, *because of the Angels*, is this; The Great Church held an Opinion that the Angels fell in Love with Women. This fancy Saint *Paul* discreetly catches, and uses it as an Argument to perswade them to modesty.

2. The Grant of a place, is not good by the Canon-Law before a man be dead; upon this ground some mischief might be plotted against him in present possession, by poisoning, or some other way. Upon

the fame reafon a Contract made with a Woman during her husband's life, was not valid.

3. Men are not troubled to hear a Man difpraifed, becaufe they know, though he be naught, there's worth in others. But Women are mightily troubled to hear any of them spoken againft as if the Sex it felf were guilty of fome unworthinefs.

4. Women and Princes muft both truft fomebody; and they are happy, or unhappy according to the defert of thofe under whofe hands they fall. If a man knows how to manage the favour of a Lady, her Honour is fafe, and fo is a Princes.

5. An Opinion grounded upon that, *Genefis* 6. *The Sons of God faw the Daughters of Men that they were fair.*

Year.

1. 'TWas the manner of the Jews (if the Year did not fall out right, but that it was dirty for the people to come up to *Jerufalem*, at the Feaft of the Paffover; or that their Corn was not ripe for their firft Fruits) to intercalate a Month, and fo to have, as it were, two *Februarys;* thrufting up the Year ftill higher, *March* into *April*'s place, *April* into *May*'s place, &c. Whereupon it is impoffible for us to know when our Saviour was born, or when he dy'd.

2. The Year is either the year of the Moon, or the Year of the Sun; there's not above Eleven days difference. Our moveable Feafts are according to the Year of the Moon; elfe they fhould be fixt.

3. Though they reckon Ten days fooner beyond Sea; yet it does not follow their Spring is fooner than ours; we keep the fame time in natural things, and their Ten days fooner, and our Ten days later in thofe things mean the felf fame time; juft as Twelve *Sous* in French, are Ten Pence in Englifh.

4. The lengthening of days is not fuddenly perciev'd till they are grown a pretty deal longer, becaufe the Sun, though it be in a Circle, yet it feems for a while to go in a right Line. For take a Segment of a great Circle efpecially, and you fhall doubt whether it be

ſtraight or no. But when that Sun is got paſt that Line, then you preſently percieve the days are lengthened. Thus it is in the Winter and Summer Solſtice; which is indeed the true reaſon of them.

5. The Eclipſe of the Sun is, when it is new Moon; the Eclipſe of the Moon when 'tis full. They ſay *Dionyſius* was converted by the Eclipſe that happened at our Saviour's Death, becauſe it was neither of theſe, and ſo could not be natural.

Zelots.

1. ONE would wonder Chriſt ſhould whip the Buyers and Sellers out of the Temple, and no Body offer to reſiſt him (conſidering what Opinion they had of him.) But the reaſon was, they had a Law, that whoſoever ſhould profane *Sanctitatem Dei, aut Templi;* the Holineſs of God, or the Temple, before Ten perſons, 'twas lawful for any of them to kill him, or to do any thing this ſide killing him; as Whipping him, or the like. And hence it was, that when one ſtruck our Saviour before the Judge where it was not lawful to ſtrike (as it is not with us at this day) he only replies; If I have ſpoken evil, bear witneſs of the Evil; but if well why ſmiteſt thou me? He ſays nothing againſt their ſmiting him, in caſe he had been guilty of ſpeaking Evil, that is Blaſphemy; and they could have prov'd it againſt him. They that put this law in Execution were called Zelots; but afterwards they committed many Villainies.

FINIS.

J. & W. Rider, Printers, London.

Alex. Murray and Son's

LIST OF WORKS

PUBLISHED AND TO BE PUBLISHED.

English Reprints.	2—5
Sir W. Scott's Poetical Romances.	6
Outlines of Scottish History.	6
Topographical.	7
Classic English Writers.	8

LONDON:
30, QUEEN SQUARE, W.C.
1868.

English Reprints.

CHIEFLY IN SIXPENNY AND SHILLING VOLUMES.

The 'English Reprints' have proved a greater success than I anticipated. More copies of the several works issued have been already sold in the open market, than have been produced, in the same time, by any Printing Club, by subscription.

I am thereby encouraged to go on with the series, and I trust bring out, during the remainder of the year, the works announced pages 4 and 5: so that the first year's issue will contain specimens of

16th Cent. Ascham, Bp. Latimer, Gascoigne, Gosson, Lilly, E. Webbe, and Sir Philip Sidney. 7
17th Cent. Bp. Earle, Milton, Villiers, Duke of Buckingham, and Selden. 4
18th Cent. Addison. . . . . 1—1

If therefore any go about ignorant of thus much of our literature they only will be to blame: for it seems impossible to reprint these works cheaper. Strange to say, their cheapness militates at present against their universal sale: but this obstacle will doubtless melt away as the series become more known.

The question of binding has been a perplexity. The books—choicely produced as they are—are too small in bulk and size to repay binding in single volumes. To publish them, several bound together, in the order of their issue—unconnected and diverse as they are in subject, purpose and character,—seems unmeaning and purposeless; would often tax the purchaser with works he did not desire; and would fetter the use in large quantities of any particular work, for class study, debating societies and the like. As nothing can foster more the fresh and increasing general study in our language and literature, than the free circulation throughout the country, of *cheap* as well as *accurate* texts; the 'English Reprints' will continue to be issued separately, at the general prices originally announced. What therefore remains is to provide cases to contain six of the works, leaving to each one, unfettered choice in their selection. These cases will be obtainable, in the same way as the books themselves, after the 7th of May.

The 'English Reprints' being thus current, all can now most readily avail themselves of the capabilities of English, as a gymnasium of intellect, an instrument of culture; or passing within the Treasure-house of the language, possess themselves of the stored-up precious wealth of thought and fact, the accumulation therein of century after century.

The *Areopagitica* is already read in King's College and other schools other suitable texts will doubtless be similarly utilized.

I desire to call attention to *Euphues*. It was last published in 1636. The present impression will contain the two parts, originally issued separately in 1579 and 1580; will be printed from copies supposed to be unique and will form a volume of between 400 and 500 pages. This work represents a fashion of expression in the Elizabethan age, and gave a word *Euphuism* to the English language. An acquaintance with it, is essential to an accurate knowledge of the literature of the time of Shakespeare.

In conclusion, I tender my sincere thanks to some for their zealous advocacy of the series: and can but hope it may appear to others worthy of like approval and encouragement.

23 April, 1868. EDWARD ARBER.

P.S. That there are no further Sixpenny issues this year, is purely accidental

English Reprints.

CAREFULLY EDITED BY

EDWARD ARBER.

Associate, King's College, London, F·R G.S., &c.

Ready.

1. JOHN MILTON.

(1) A decree of Starre-Chamber, concerning Printing, made the eleuenth day of July last past. London, 1637.

(2) An Order of the Lords and Commons assembled in Parliament for the regulating of Printing, &c. London, 14 June, 1643.

(3) *AREOPAGITICA*; A speech of Mr. John Milton for the liberty of Vnlicenc'd Printing, to the Parlament of England. London [24 November], 1644. **Sixpence.**

2. HUGH LATIMER, Bp. of Worcester.

SERMON ON THE PLOUGHERS. A notable Sermon of ye reuerende father Master Hughe Latimer, whiche he preached in ye Shrouds at paules churche in London, on the xviii daye of Januarye. ¶ The yere of oure Loorde MDXLviii. **Sixpence.**

3. STEPHEN GOSSON, Stud. Oxon.

(1) *THE SCHOOLE OF ABUSE.* Conteining a pleasaunt invective against Poets, Pipers, Plaiers, Jesters, and such like Caterpillers of a Commonwealth; Setting up the Flagge of Defiance to their mischievous exercise, and ouerthrowing their Bulwarkes, by Prophane Writers, Naturall reason, and common experience. A discourse as pleasaunt for gentlemen that fauour learning, as profitable for all that wyll follow vertue. London [August ?] 1579.

(2) *AN APOLOGIE OF THE SCHOOLE OF ABUSE,* against Poets, Pipers, and their Excusers. London, [December ?] 1579. **Sixpence.**

4. Sir PHILIP SIDNEY.

AN APOLOGIE FOR POETRIE. Written by the right noble, vertuous, and learned Sir Phillip Sidney, Knight. London, 1595. **Sixpence.**

English Reprints—In Preparation.

5. E. WEBBE, Chief Master Gunner.

The rare and most vvonderful thinges which **Edward** Webbe an Englishman borne, hath seene and passed in his troublesome trauailes, in the Citties of Ierusalem, Dammasko, Bethelem, and Galely: and in the Landes of Iewrie, Egipt, Gtecia, Russia, and in the land of Prester Iohn. Wherein is set foorth his extreame slauerie sustained many yeres togither, in the Gallies and wars of the great Turk against the Landes of Persia, Tartaria, Spaine, and Portugall, with the manner of his releasement, and comming into Englande in May last. London, 1590.   Sixpence. [*May* 1.

6. JOHN SELDEN.

TABLE TALK: being the Discourses of John Selden Esq.; or his Sence of various Matters of Weight and High Consequence relating especially to Religion and State. London, 1689.   One Shilling. [*June* 1.

7. ROGER ASCHAM.

TOXOPHILUS. The schole of shooting conteyned in tvvo bookes. To all Gentlemen and yomen of Englande, pleasaunte for theyr pastime to rede, and profitable for theyr use to folow, both in war and peace. London, 1545.   One Shilling. [*July* 1.

8. JOSEPH ADDISON.

CRITICISM OF MILTON'S PARADISE LOST. From the *Spectator*: being its Saturday issues between 31 December, 1711, and 3 May, 1712. London.
   One Shilling. [*Aug.* 1.
No Issue in September.

9. JOHN LILLY.

(1) ¶ *EUPHUES. THE ANATOMY OF WIT*. Verie pleasaunt for all Gentlemen to read, and most necessarie to remember. Wherein are contained the delightes that Wit followeth in his youth by the pleasantnesse of loue, and the happinesse he reapeth in age, by the perfectnesse of Wisedome. London, 1579.

(2) ¶ *EUPHUES AND HIS ENGLAND*. Containing his voyage and aduentures, myxed with sundry pretie discourses of honest Loue, the Discription of the Countrey, the Court, and the manners of that Isle. Delightful to be read, and nothing hurtfull to be regarded: wher-in there is small offence by lightnesse giuen to the wise, and lesse occasion of loosenes proffered to the wanton. London, 1580.   Four Shillings. [*Oct.* 1.

English Reprints—In Preparation.

10. GEORGE VILLIERS, Second Duke of Buckingham.

THE REHEARSAL. As it was Acted at the Theatre Royal. London, 1672. With the readings of subsequent editions up to the author's death, and the passages parodied. **One Shilling.** [*Nov.* 1.

11. GEORGE GASCOIGNE, Esquire.

(1) A Remembravnce of the wel imployed life, and godly end of George Gaskoigne, Esquire, who deceassed at Stalmford in Lincoln shire, the 7 of October 1577. The reporte of GEOR WHETSTONS, Gent an eye witnes of his Godly and charitable End in this world. London 1577.

(2) Certayne notes of Instruction concerning the making of verse or ryme in English, vvritten at the request of Master *Edouardo Donati.* 1575.

(3) *THE STEELE GLAS.* A Satyre compiled by George Gasscoigne Esquire [Written between April 1575 and April 1576]. Togither with

(4) *THE COMPLAYNT OF PHYLOMENE.* An Elegye compyled by George Gasscoigne Esquire [between April 1562 and 3rd April 1576.] London 1576.
One Shilling. [*Nov.* 15.

12. JOHN EARLE, successively Bishop of Worcester and Salisbury.

MICRO-COSMOGRAPHIE. or, a Peece of the World discovered, in Essayes and Characters. London 1628. With the additions in subsequent editions during the Author's life time. **One Shilling.** [*Dec.* 1

Copies will be sent post free by the publishers on the receipt of—
> Seven stamps for Sixpenny copies;
> Fourteen stamps for Shilling copies;
> Fifty-four stamps for *Euphues.*

Uncut copies can be had, at the same prices. It will be convenient, if they are ordered in advance.

Handsome cases, in best roan and cloth, Roxburghe style, to contain six of the 'Reprints,' will be ready after the 7th of May.

One Shilling each; post free, Fourteen stamps.

Sir Walter Scott's
Poetical Romances,

with notes.

In sixpenny volumes, crown 8vo., 128 pages, by post, seven stamps.

1. The Lady of the Lake.
2. The Lord of the Isles.
3. The Lay of the Last Minstrel.
4. Marmion—Flodden-field.

Complete in one volume, 512 pp., Cloth, Half-a-Crown; by Post, 2s. 9d.

5. The Scott Epistles, Waterloo, &c.
6. Rokeby—Barnard Castle.
7. Bridal of Triermain.
8. Ballads, Songs, Poems, &c.

Complete in one volume, 512 pp., Cloth, Half-a-Crown; by Post, 2s. 9d.

Outlines of Scottish History,

BY

Alexander Murray.

PART I.

From the earliest authentic records, to the close of the reign of David Bruce.

Fcap. 18mo., Cloth, 200 pp. Two Shillings; by Post, 2s. 2d.

THE UPPER WARD OF LANARKSHIRE.
Described and Delineated.

1. Archæology, &c.: by G. V. IRVING, F.S.A., Scot.
2. Statistics and Topography: by ALEXANDER MURRAY.

Maps and Illustrations. 3 vols.

*Large paper edition, Demy 4to., Cloth, £5 5 0
or in Demy 8vo., Cloth, £3 3 0*

ALL THAT IS WORTH SEEING IN SCOTLAND
Described by ALEXANDER MURRAY.
Fcp. 8vo., Cloth, 5s.; by Post, 5s. 3d.

HAND-BOOKS FOR SCOTLAND.
By ALEXANDER MURRAY.

Maps, &c. Fcp. 16mo. Neat Stiff Covers.

Sixpence each; by Post, Seven Stamps; except * which are Fourpence each; by Post, Five Stamps.

THE CLYDE SERIES.

*1. THE CLYDE, the KELVIN, GOVAN, RENFREW, BOWLING.
*2. DUMBARTON, PORT-GLASGOW, HELENSBURGH, the GARE-LOCH.
*3. KILCREGGAN, ARROCHAR, LOCH-GOIL, KILMUN, DUNOON.
*4. GREENOCK, GOUROCK, WEMYSS-BAY, LARGS, MILLPORT.
*5. INNELLAN, ROTHESAY, MOUNT-STEWART, KAMES, ISLE OF BUTE.
6. ARDROSSAN, BRODICK, LAMLASH, LOCH-RANZA, ARRAN.

Complete in one volume. Cloth. Half-a-Crown; by Post, 2s. 8d.

THE HIGHLAND SERIES.

7. INVERARY and LOCH-AWE; by TARBET, ARROCHAR, and GLEN-CROE; LOCH-GOILHEAD, KILMUN, KYLES OF BUTE, LOCH-FYNE.
8. OBAN, STAFFA, and IONA; by the CRINAN CANAL, SOUND OF JURA, the SLATE ISLES, and the SOUND OF MULL.
9. BALLACHULISH, FORT WILLIAM, ald INVERNESS; by Coach Route and Steamer, BEN-NEVIS, and CALEDONIAN CANAL.
10. The PERTHSHIRE HIGHLANDS; by DOUNE, CALLANDER, the TROSSACHS, LOCH-KATRINE, LOCH-EARN, and CRIEFF.

Complete in one volume. Cloth. Half-a-Crown; by post, 2s. 8d.

11. The Railway to BALLOCH, LOCH-LOMOND, BEN-LOMOND, GLEN-FALLOCH, STRATHFILLAN, KING'S HOUSE, GLENCOE.
12. The Dee-side—ABERDEEN to BANCHORY, BALLATER, LOCH-NA-GAR, BALMORAL CASTLE, and CASTLETON-BRAEMAR.
13. The LAND of BURNS—ALLOWAY KIRK, the BONNY DOON, IRVINE, MAUCHLINE, MOSSGIEL, ELLISLAND, DUMFRIES.

CLASSIC ENGLISH WRITERS.

IN SHILLING PARTS, CROWN OCTAVO.

HENRY HALLAM.

View of the State of Europe during the Middle Ages.

PART I.
FRANCE—THE FEUDAL SYSTEM. [*Ready.*

PART II.
SPAIN—ITALY—GERMANY. [*Ready.*

PART III.
GREEKS—SARACENS—ECCLESIASTICAL POWER. [*May* 1.

PART IV.
CONSTITUTIONAL HISTORY OF ENGLAND, TO RICHARD III. [*May* 15.

PART V.
STATE OF SOCIETY IN THE MIDDLE AGES. [*June* 1.

The entire work, handsomely bound in one volume, 840 pages,
Will be ready on June 1. Price, Six Shillings.
Postage—of Parts, 2d.; of Volumes, 6d.

LONDON: ALEX. MURRAY & SON,
30, QUEEN SQUARE, W.C.